AF492278

PRAISE FOR STAY SWEET

Stay Sweet is like a pecan pie for the soul. It will transport you, delight you, and may just transform you!

— DR. ADRIENNE MACIAIN, AUTHOR OF
SPARK GENIUS: CREATIVE FLOW UNLEASHED

Reading Chris Chandler's charming collection of stories is like cozying up by the fire, a hot toddy in your mug, a handmade 'grandma' quilt tucked around you, and the voices of ancestors and sisterhood embracing you. It is a hug, a warm embrace. These quirky tales of family and a deep love will warm your heart. It's hard to put down!

— JESSICA GOLDMUNTZ STOKES AUTHOR
OF *SEEKING CLARITY IN THE LABYRINTH: A
DAUGHTER'S JOURNEY THROUGH
ALZHEIMER'S*

Grab a coffee in your favorite mug with a blanket and curl up for the hug that awaits you. Stay Sweet is the perfect cozy memoir to warm your heart.

— NICOLE HARKIN AUTHOR OF *TILTING: A
MEMOIR*

Here's a rare treat — a really good memoir about a happy childhood. Those two things are usually mutually exclusive, but Chris Chandler's evocative writing takes the reader right into the safe, laughter-infused world of the extended family of her youth.

— LISA JONES, AUTHOR OF *BROKEN: A LOVE STORY*

Reading Stay Sweet feels like walking into a happy family party where multiple generations are busy celebrating their love, respect, and devotion to each other. Think the opposite of Eugene O'Neill's Tyrone clan. Chandler's playful, witty, and insightful voice is the perfect companion on this charming and eclectic adventure to meet the unforgettable May Tennille Donnelly, her beloved grandmother, and the other members of her unconventional tribe. I just wanted to keep on reading.

— DR. CHRISTINE M. TRACY, AUTHOR OF *THE NEWSPHERE* AND *THE MYSTIC AS EVERYMAN*

STAY SWEET: TALES OF QUIRKY SOUTHERN LOVE

CHRIS CHANDLER

Red Thread Publishing LLC. 2023

Write to **info@redthreadbooks.com** if you are interested in publishing with Red Thread Publishing. Learn more about publications or foreign rights acquisitions of our catalog of books: www.redthreadbooks.com

Copyright © 2023 by Chris Chandler

All rights reserved.

No part of this book may be reproduced in any form or by any electronic or mechanical means, including information storage and retrieval systems, without written permission from the author, except for the use of brief quotations in a book review.

Paperback ISBN: 978-1-955683-64-7

Ebook ISBN: 978-1-955683-65-4

Cover Design: Jodi Tripp www.joditripp.com

For May Tennille Donnelly:
December 13, 1919-May 28, 2012
My grandmother, my friend, my cheerleader.

For Will and Bridget:
Because she also loved you so much.

For Will, George, Catherine, and Mary Rose:
So her memory lives on for you.

CONTENTS

1

BACKSEAT PEW

The best thing that could happen to me when I was a child was for my grandmother May to say, "Let's go get a Coca-Cola and go for a ride."

I mean a real Coke. One with lots of sugar. The kind that came chilled, in a small green glass bottle. One that had to be opened with a bottle opener attached to the store counter or outside on the wall, pulled from a silver-lidded chest cooler spilling cold air when you opened the top and reached in. Or from a drink machine with a long narrow glass door, the bottles on their sides in a tall, vertical row. These rides with May often included other family members. My favorites were the women-only rides.

It didn't matter if we were going across town or across the country; the first order of business was to stop at a filling station (that's a gas station for those of you who don't speak Southern) to get Cokes and packages of fluorescent orange cheese and peanut butter crackers for everyone.

This wasn't just an unquestioned and essential part of the ritual. It *was* the ritual. We'd no more go on a ride without these items than any other ceremony would take place without its consecrated elements. Cokes and peanut-butter-cheese crackers were our road trip Eucharist. Necessary preparation for the fun to begin: being together, talking and laughing.

My version of paradise is sitting in the backseat of a wood-paneled station wagon next to May, or my great-grandmother, or any selection of the women in my family, sipping a "co-cola," a soft hand patting my knee, someone calling me Angel or Sugar. My backseat pew in this church of women. I settle in and wait because the best part is about to get started.

No matter where we were going or where we ended up, wherever we might stop to sit on a bench or in the car to look at the view, it was all about the stories. Life was one long story—the daffy things my great-grandmother did and said; the numerous times May's back bumper got a bit too close to a tree; the time May and her friend bought and fried a freshly killed but poorly plucked chicken for a picnic. The stories that tell me about myself: who and where I came from, where I belong, the place and people of my first home.

On days I feel troubled, in need of comfort, physical or mental, I call upon these women and their tales. You might think I conjure them with a dance or song or prayer but it's far simpler than that. All I have to do is pop the top off a bottle of Coke and tear into a pack of crackers. If it can be done while rolling down the road, so much the better.

Whether we're aware of it or not, we all participate in stories. We watch the news, read novels, listen to true crime podcasts, go to the movies, read the newspaper or magazines. We nudge our friend and say, "Oh, boy! Have I ever got something to tell you!"

We narrate our lives to our friends and family and prompt them to do the same when we ask, "How was your day?"

Our brains are meaning-making machines and one of the ways we make sense of things is through story. Storytelling is in our nature. It's the oldest way humans have for preserving history, passing on legacies and understanding our place in the world. We employ story to entertain, communicate, sell, convince, sway. But most importantly, to connect.

∾

Over the past few years, my family has gathered annually at the beach. One of my favorite things to do is to wander downstairs to the condo my aunt and uncle are staying in. Because I know if I go in there and sit at the table, it'll be maybe five minutes before something in the conversation reminds someone of a story. Then out it will come, and we're off.

I want nothing more than to sit down with you, listen to your stories, discover the people, places and events that populate them, and hear what you make of them. And to spin a tale or two for you.

Stories. These are mine.

2

DOWNTOWN MILLEDGEVILLE

The little town of Milledgeville, Georgia and surrounding Baldwin County was home to at least four generations on both sides of my family and is my birthplace. Although I only lived there or nearby until age four, I returned there to my grandparents' homes until my early fifties. It's an ancestral and heart home.

Milledgeville has a historic downtown with wide streets and pull-in parking on both sides. The buildings are brick and wood. Many hold large plate glass windows that allow passersby to gaze into the shops and offices. "Going to town" was a favorite thing for me to do with May, my maternal grandmother.

Milledgeville was designed and settled as Georgia's capital in 1803, a role it served for sixty-one years. The old columned two-story governor's mansion sits in town on a slightly elevated lot, frilly with white and pink dogwood trees and bright pink azaleas during the spring.

A few blocks away, St. Stephens Episcopal Church sits among the shade of tall pine trees. Its dark brown wood exterior is somber and plain. Arched windows punctuate the long lap boards that run around it. It echoes inside, all that space and not much to soften it. The wooden floor still holds prints of horses' hooves from Sherman's March to the Sea when he stopped there and used the church as a stable. Long wooden pews fill the floor. It smells of dusty hymnals, old wood. Years of organ music and voices singing permeate the walls.

During my childhood years, across and down the street from the church, the Western Auto Store sat on the corner. This is where Billy, my maternal grandfather, works. It smells of bitter rubber—the tires of mowers and bicycles and autos. It holds tools and riding mowers and grills, automobile batteries, bolts and screws. I love to go visit him there while he's working and sit on the mowers, pretending to drive them. I run my fingers through the tassels that hang from the kid's bicycle handles where the bikes sit lined up, waiting to be bought.

Billy always carries a small receipt book in his pocket with a slip of carbon between the pages. Sometimes when he's home, he reaches into his shirt pocket, plucks it out, and hands it to me along with the ink pen that also lives there. One of my favorite things is to pretend to take orders for meals, or to write up a pretend purchase, total it, and then ceremoniously rip off the top page for my customer, seeing an exact though fainter copy underneath. My stomach flips with the wizardry of producing a duplicate.

Hank, who also works at the store, is usually there when I come in. He wears dungarees or navy blue coveralls, his name, "Hank," in black cursive on a white patch on his chest. He has a huge smile and white, straight teeth. His hair is cut in a flat top. He has long, wiry legs. "Hey, Sugar!" he shouts as I walk in the door. "You walk just like your Daddy." I beam. I like being like my daddy. I like being seen. Being known.

After seeing Billy and Hank, I go to the business office in the back of the store to visit with Polly. She sits at her desk in the small space behind the glass counter that holds the birthstone rings, a color for every month, wedged into foam slits that hold them upright in the display. Her hair is held tight in its coif with hairspray I can smell, her lipstick red, her hair getting a little grayer each year, her tummy pooching a little more underneath the belt that circles the waist of her skirt.

"Come over here and see me, darlin'," she drawls. Even though I've been greeting her in this same place, same way my entire life, I have an initial moment of shyness when I first see her again, even though I thrill at her attention.

I stare longingly at the rings in the case, especially the purple one, the amethyst, my birthstone. I never ask to try one on. I never ask if I can have one as a gift. I never think to buy one with my own money. I just look at them and wish.

A block away is my Grandaddy Chandler's office. He sells propane and says things to me like "now we're cooking with gas" and "cat snagged my purple blue jeans," which I understand to be some sort of exclamation but which otherwise totally puzzles me, like a lot of other things he says.

Grandaddy is impressed and obsessed with typewriters. His office holds a few of these amazing machines, and I am allowed to feed paper into them, then turn the clicking roller to get the paper to just the right spot, push the keys, hear the clack, clack, clack, and see words magically appear on the page. I perform more duplication with carbon paper and learn the miracles of correction fluid and tape. Sometimes I type too fast and cause several of the metal arms to clump together up by the paper. I get my hands inky prying them apart. Sometimes the ribbon twists or runs out of ink and I feel official when I get to fix it myself.

Rose's 5 & 10 is a long narrow store that smells like bubblegum and mellowed wood. It is full of trinkets and costume jewelry, a great place for me to spend fifty cents on plastic beaded bracelets, coloring books or barrettes. The wooden floorboards run longways down the narrow aisles and squeak as you walk.

May often does her grocery shopping at Joiner's Market, a small grocery store in the heart of town. Joiner's has a butcher in back, making the store smell like blood and raw meat. Not my favorite place to go.

The reward for tolerating the smells at Joiner's is a trip next door to Kirkpatrick's Bakery. Its store front is all glass. From the sidewalk, I can see inside the store to the two long glass cases that hold bread, pastries, cookies, and cakes. On the right side of the store and close to the front window is a display of large wedding cakes, tier upon tier, decorated with thick white icing and a plastic figure of a bride and groom on top. I am certain all my wedding cake dreams were formed standing in front of Kirkpatrick's, looking at their sample wedding cakes.

At Kirkpatrick's I always get a gingerbread man with raisin buttons, eyes, and mouth. It never occurs to me to desire anything else. The eating of my gingerbread man is ritualistic. I eat the buttons first, then the eyes, the mouth, the feet, the hands, the head, then the body. No exceptions. It is pleasing, this routine, the steps.

Pulling open the door to the bakery, my nose fills with scents of flour, sugar, yeast. The air inside is warm. I order my gingerbread man, listen to the crinkle of the white wax paper square used to pick it up, and reach for it over the large glass counter.

Sometimes May and I make a special trip to Thigpen's Shoe store. We call it Pigpen's, a silly twist on the name I'm sure the Thigpen family has heard more than enough of in their lifetime. I sit down on the naugahyde bench and wait for the salesman to come over with his silver metal measuring device. He gently takes my heel and places it into the heel cup, arranges my foot so it is straight, slides the lever on the side that measures the width of my foot, looks at the strange intersection of lines and announces my shoe size.

I love the anticipation as he goes in and out of the back room to get shoes, my insides jumping as I wonder if he'll find my size in the shoes I've just picked out and am now sure I can't live without. Usually I'm lucky. We drive home, me on the front seat beside May, my old shoes in the shoebox, the new ones on my feet. I'm so proud, I can't stop looking at them. I'm certain I never want to take them off and wish I could sleep in them.

One summer May buys me a pair of sandals with pink, white, and blue straps that cross over the foot near the toes. One of them accidentally gets scooped up with the laundry, goes through the washer and dryer, comes out shriveled and curled. I cry. When we go back to try to replace them, they don't have more in my size.

May has a pair of rust-colored suede pumps that also inadvertently make their way into the washing machine but they come out looking better than ever, so much so that she intentionally washes them in the machine occasionally. It is from her I learn that almost anything can be washed in either the washing machine or dishwasher.

I am fascinated with Eberhardt's Photography Studio. It is on one of the main downtown streets with large plate glass windows across the front, set into heavy wooden frames. Portraits stand on easels turned toward the window. I stop and stare, wondering who the people are, and if my photo will ever be there on display.

Grant's Jeweler's also sells silver—trays, cups to be engraved, pitchers, napkin rings, serving dishes. Silver is a gift of choice for weddings, graduations, and new babies. I look longingly at the shining objects, thinking about the day when such things might be gifted to me.

This town is the backdrop for most of my family history, the place my great-grandparents, grandparents, parents were born and lived out their days. A place where we are recognized, known for who we are and who we are connected to. A common question is "Who are your people?" Your people. My people. They are the Tennilles and Donnellys, the Chandlers, the Tomlins and Richardsons. That's where I fit. I can point easily to where I belong.

~

I've moved a lot over the years, especially in my adult life. I've lived in the Southeast, Northeast, West and Pacific-Northwest—and experienced the micro-cultures that exist in the US. Each region comes with its own ways of doing things, foods, approaches to life, accents, aphorisms, climates, bugs, preferred vehicles, and favored dog breeds. I'm grateful for the way these different homes have informed me, introduced me to new people and showed me new ways to live. I don't regret it.

But there's also a part of me that is sad to have left a place that was home to my family for so long. Sad to have broken a certain continuity of place and home. And perhaps this is one reason why carrying these stories, making sure that home continues to reside inside, is so important to me.

3

OUR LITTLE SECRET

I'm at May and Billy's house with my parents, probably over the holidays. I'm five or six, young enough that *they* —my parents— still try to make me go to bed at some ridiculously early hour. Torture.

I'm in the back bedroom, down the hallway and around the corner, at the other end of May and Billy's L-shaped house.

Even though I am as far from the living room as I can possibly be, the house isn't large and my location doesn't stop me hearing the sounds of voices, laughter, ice tinkling in glasses, the occasional clink of the silver bracelets May wears on her wrist as I lie in the dark room. I twist around in the sheets, move my pillow to the other end of the bed. I hang my head over the side of the bed and slowly roll off backwards until my feet hit the low trundle bed below. I sing. But I don't fall asleep.

I can make out distinct voices. Sometimes I sneak down the hallway and peek around the corner, watching and listening, eventually giving up and creeping back to the bedroom.

Billy laughs, a heh-heh-heh sound, low, slow. In my mind I can see the way he shows his teeth when he laughs, the way his lips pull back but his teeth stay together, Cheshire Cat-like.

Betty, May's sister, calls people Angel and My Baby. Her laugh, throaty, tumbles out easily. She's pretty, dressed in pastels, her delicate fingers ending in fingernails painted pearl pink, her scent delicate, powdery, light. The bracelet she wears is loose around her wrist. The charms sing when she moves her arm.

May's laugh is slightly higher than her sister's. She pinches the bridge of her nose when things really get funny, when she gets, as she calls it, "tickled." When laughter overtakes her, she puts one hand across her stomach, leans over slightly and rocks with hilarity. Sometimes there is lipstick on her teeth. Sometimes she snorts.

I hate being back here alone. Because they are telling stories —I know it—and there is nothing I love more. I want to be in the living room with them, mostly quiet, listening and watching, tucked under someone's arm or in a lap. I want to hear the stories, the things they talk about. I want to be a part of it.

The "back" bedroom is what we call the room I'm in. The one that used to be my Uncle Ricky's, my mom's younger brother.

It has a dresser with a top drawer still full of trinkets that belong to Ricky, little pieces of his life as a teenager in that room. A colored stripe never sewn onto his Georgia Military College uniform, a single marble, a key. I like to open the drawer and look at them, push them around with my finger, examine the little still life of him.

One wall in the room is lined with cabinets below and bookshelves above. They are full of *National Geographic* magazines and hardback books about WWII history, Billy's passion.

I sigh with boredom. But there's hope, because here's what I know: at some point, May will sneak away from everyone on the pretense of refilling her drink or tidying up empty glasses. Sure enough, there she is in the doorway. "Hey, Shug," she whispers, creeping into the room toward me. With her hug, I breathe in powder, hairspray and cinnamon gum. She has Oreos on a small plate, a glass of milk, an Archie comic book, and a flashlight.

We have the perfect hiding place for it all—under the trundle bed. We have done this before, so I know how it works. We pulled the trundle out at bedtime and left it low so there is a space under the higher part of the bed. The perfect place for hiding contraband. And for me, it's fun to crawl into the small space with my treats, cozy up, snack and read.

May knows my mom and dad will object to her smuggling me into the party so she brings some of the party to me.

"It is," she says, smiling, "our little secret."

4

CIRCLE OF WOMEN

Belonging. It looks like this. Sitting in the front yard with May and her sister Betty, hand sewing doll clothes.

Learning to embroider by their sides. Being gently schooled in the stitches: the blanket stitch to go around the edges of a piece; French knots, my favorites, those delicate little buds of thread; running stitches to make a long line. Something so delicate and delicious about them, like tiny pieces of candy on the fabric. I remember the off-white of the material, shapes of flowers and birds and swirling stems. Colors of fern green and turquoise, fuchsia and gold.

"Angel, can you thread this needle for me?" May or Betty would ask me. The thrill of this thing my young eyes could do, a competence, a way I could contribute.

The sampler of stitches I sewed. The one May framed and hung on the wall, a small square on cream fabric, the flowers delicate and pastel, marks I made treasured, framed and displayed. My initials, CC, in the corner.

Belonging looks like never being left out of the circle of women. Being there for it all. The 10 p.m. shopping trips to

Marshall's; late night gatherings in pjs; all of us balled up together on chairs and couches; laughter, so much laughter. I'm sure there were adult discussions I was never a part of but I don't ever remember being pushed out of a conversation; I don't remember the hush that comes over a conversation when people don't want kids to hear. I was never included in things that were too mature for me. I was exquisitely protected from anything like that and yet the talk and stories flowed easily.

It meant being included, taken in and related to as a person —not pushed to the side because I was a child. Or a girl. It meant never being laughed at when I expressed my opinion. There was a comfort, an ease of being. An ease of being among.

5

SO SICK

"Will you please come get us? I want to see that great pediatrician, Dr. Schwartz, in Macon," Mom pleads to May and Billy.

It's July 1963. I'm seventeen months old.

The trip from Milledgeville to Charlotte, North Carolina, where we were living, was 250 miles. May and Billy were both still working and had full lives. But "they got there as fast as a car could possibly carry them," Mom says. "Then they turned around and drove us straight to Macon to that doctor."

The prior fall, I had developed a mystery illness, repeatedly spiking dangerously high fevers, and often some combination of pneumonia, strep and tonsillitis. I'd be rushed to the infirmary of the Army base where we were living and sometimes admitted to the hospital, only to be treated, released, and eventually become sick again.

~

Dr. Schwartz's recommendation? Remove tonsils. Now.

In 1963, people were still afraid of a tonsillectomy. The surgery and anesthesia for children was less familiar to people, and it scared them. May and Billy and my mom and dad were scared too. But they also knew something had to be done.

As they prepared for me to have surgery the next day, word got round to family and friends. Most were supportive but, Mom says, some would call and start down the "Don't-you-know-how-dangerous-that-is?" road.

"May would hear people saying that and she'd take the phone and hang up on them. She just wasn't going to take it," Mom said.

Luckily the surgery solved everything. All my symptoms resolved, my appetite returned, I gained weight, and the naysayers were proved wrong.

May and Billy were there for me—and my parents—pacing around hospital waiting rooms, taking care of me when my mom was sick postpartum, never hesitating to help out. I suspect the memory of being taken care of, of being able to depend on people, lives in me in ways I can't even name.

Having that kind of safety net helps me feel an ease and confidence in moving through the world that can't be overestimated. As my friend recently commented, "We all need advocates." There's a giant something to being sure you have a place to land, no matter what.

6

HOW TO MAKE A DEAL WITH THE DEVIL INVOLVING JELLO SALAD

1 Wake up at 2:30 am, alone in your graduate school apartment.

2. Be horribly sick, vomit multiple times.

3. Feel miserable and afraid. Sleep with a mixing bowl by your side.

4. Lay there in the dark with the light of the bathroom glowing around the corner, the one you've left on to help you feel less alone.

5. Decide to make a deal with the Devil.

6. Swear to forever and uncomplainingly do the following if Mom or May will materialize on the spot to take care of you:

- Go to church
- Wear panty hose with high heels
- Go to brunch at the country club after church
- Eat anything in a Jello mold

7. No one appears.

8. Be uncertain whether it's fortunate or unfortunate no one appeared because now you don't have to carry out The Deal.

9. Be unsure which offering above would have been the greatest sacrifice.

10. Decide it was probably the promise to eat things in a Jello mold. (Even as a kid, you were not a Jello fan. Too sweet and what's with the jiggly, slimy texture? Even worse, you find, is Jello with lumps in it—things like grapes, apples, bananas.)

11. Remember that Tomato aspic, considered by many the crown jewel of things gelatinized, is the ultimate in gross. Though a lover of tomatoes, tomato juice makes you gag. Take tomato juice, make it into Jello, and, as some people do, add chopped veggies—and you've just come up with your worst food nightmare.

12. Be chagrined to recall there's actually a Jello salad you would (and will) eat.

13. Add it to this year's Thanksgiving menu. Because what's Thanksgiving to a Southerner without something weird in a Jello mold?

Lime Jello Salad recipe

> *1 pkg. (3 oz.) lime gelatin*
> *1 cup hot water*
> *2 small (3 oz.) packages cream cheese*
> *1 small (8oz.) can crushed pineapple*
> *1 Tablespoon sugar*
> *1 teaspoon vanilla*
> *1-6 oz. bottle 7-UP*
> *1/2 cup chopped pecans*

Dissolve gelatin in hot water. Cool. Add remaining ingredients. Put it in a Pyrex dish and chill. Cut into any size squares and serve on lettuce.

14. Be eternally grateful you don't have to wear pantyhose

while eating your Jello salad. This is more than fortunate since the only shoes you can tolerate these days are Birkenstocks and clogs.

7

NIGHT OWLS

I come from a long line of night owls. Let me tell you: it's not easy being one in a world that favors the early bird. Thankfully, I have stay-up-late/sleep-late women in my family, including Mom and May, as reminders that there's nothing wrong with me just because I regard any hour before nine a.m. unappealing for wakefulness.

When I'm a child and staying at May's house, we stay up late. Every night. We never miss watching The Tonight Show with Johnny Carson on May's little black-and-white TV in her bedroom with two short silver antennae sticking up from the back. By the time we climb into her bed, Billy is long asleep and snoring in the other bedroom.

We prop up in her queen-sized four-poster bed with spindles that reach so high they could support a canopy. The bed is always covered with something floral and pastel and lots of puffy white pillows, the cases bordered in white eyelet. She fluffs my pillow, pats the bed, and says, "Hop up here beside me, Shug." My stomach tickles in delight as I climb in beside her.

Sometimes, in these late hours, I give her a permanent with

a home kit. The smell is so pungent I'm afraid I might gag. We do this in the small bathroom connected to her bedroom, walls white, the tiles around the shower powder blue, her sitting on a stool with an old towel draped over her shoulders, me standing behind her with combs and bottles.

Or I frost her hair. She wets it down, pulls on the tight cap that comes with the kit, the one that looks like a bathing cap with small holes poked in it, and I use the provided hook, like a crochet needle, to pull hair through each hole, then apply the solution. We laugh at the sprigs of hair sticking out all over her head. She looks like a fountain with tiny twigs of hair spraying in every direction. After waiting the required amount of time, during which we watch late night TV or read magazines, she showers, rinsing off the solution and, *voilà*, another midnight hair coloring project is complete. I'm sure in my lifetime I've never seen her natural hair color, and she hasn't seen it either.

Hair perming or coloring complete, we snuggle up into her bed for the night. She doesn't like being disturbed by the phone ringing in the morning, so the last task before lights out is to pull the phone into the bathroom, cover it with a pillow and the bathmat to muffle the ring, and close the door on it. If I get up in the night to use the bathroom, I encounter a fuzzy lump attached to a cord running under the door and out to the bedroom wall.

In the days when she wore wigs—she had several—I put one on a stand and style it with the curling iron or curlers. Then I comb it out, fluff it, and hold it all in place with hairspray. She wears these wigs. In public. With my styling. Unless she is very stealthy at re-doing them, she places them on her head as-is. So either I'm a decent hairstylist, or she has no shame. I'm not sure which.

Sometimes late nights include a session of dress-up for me. I rifle through her closet, trying on clothes and shoes, scarves and necklaces, earrings and bracelets. Most fascinating to me is a pair of old-fashioned-looking boots with small buttons running up the side. I have no idea what their story is but I imagine her wearing them as a young woman. They were small enough to almost fit me in my elementary school years. When I slide my feet into them, I'm transported to some other me. Someone grown-up, dressed up, fancy and elegant.

I harbor a particular grudge against Benjamin Franklin for his "early to bed, early to rise" quote. As if a person late-to-bed, late-to-rise can't be a productive member of society. My family is one of very few I've experienced where the sleeping person is granted respect, tiptoeing, and lack of criticism.

In general, sleep is high on the list of revered experiences in my family, whether it be sleeping in, napping, or going to bed early. It's a legitimate activity, a thing to be savored, not a waste of time, as much of the world seems to think.

I still find the late night hours to be delicious. I feel safe and cozy when the rest of the house and world outside my door is quiet, when everyone else is asleep and I'm tucked in bed with a book or puttering quietly. The same way I felt on all those late nights with May.

8

CHEERING SECTION

The distance between walkers has spread considerably by Mile 22 on Day 1 of the Susan G. Komen fundraising walk. Kate is the one walker from the group of local women I have trained with who remain with me.

As she and I approach the Mile 22 aid station, six volunteers are there, but no other walkers. We have the place to ourselves. As we approach the table where the workers sit, all six jump to their feet, clap their hands, cheer and holler encouragement like we are heroes.

"Woo hoo!" they shriek. "You're doing such a good job! Thanks for all your hard work!"

We are grateful for the support, but also a little self-conscious. All we've done is walk a really long way and raise a little money.

We smile, accept high fives, have some water and a banana, and make our way back onto the course, eager to reach the stadium where we'll pitch our tent, have dinner, and sleep for the night.

I turn to Kate, "Boy, that felt great, didn't it? I could use a cheering section like that all the time. Can't you just imagine it?

Someone in your kitchen jumping up and down, clapping and shouting, 'Woo hoo! You did such a great job handling that tantrum! Way to go! You're so strong!'"

We both laugh. She has a teenager. I still have preschool age kids. We both could use the support.

As we walk in silence, putting one tired foot in front of the other, memories rise up of other times I've needed support.

I remember how my face burned hot the day I lost the student council election in seventh grade. I walked through the hallways after school tearing down my campaign posters, the ones I had thought were so smart and clever, which now seemed so stupid. I cringed when I thought back to my speech, the one I had given to all my classmates so confidently from the auditorium stage. But they had chosen someone else.

On that day, I could hardly wait to make it home, climb the stairs to my bedroom, close the door, and plop down onto the bright, flowered comforter on my bed. I picked up the phone and called May. Cried about how disappointed I felt. How rejected.

"Oh Shug! They don't know what they missed out on by not electing you. Don't you worry! I know you did a great job up there speaking. And those posters! You told me all about them and they sounded just great. It's their loss. You know I love you."

I *did* have my own cheering section!

May was the one who could always be depended on to tell me I was doing a great job. Whether it was taking my side in a spat with a parent, buoying me in the moment of disappointment when I lost that election, or the times when I didn't get asked out by my latest crush, she believed in me, cheered for me, and told me over and over again how much she loved me.

"You sweet thing you." May often said this to me. When she reached out her arms for a hug. When I called her on the phone for no particular reason at all. "Stay sweet," were her parting words on phone calls. These were her unique ways of saying "I love you."

"You sweet thing you." My mom now says at the end of our phone calls or in a text. Both of us remembering May. My mom's words keep me feeling embraced, encouraged, and cheered on.

9

MURMUR

Murmur. That's the word that keeps coming to mind. Comforting and soft.

A word that sounds like what it is: light, whispery, a breeze fluttering my hair. It's how it sounds when I sit in your lap, my head on your chest. I feel your chest rising and falling, feel warmth on my cheek. Your words vibrate through your skin, your chest cavity, a humming that makes me close my eyes or stare off into the distance. Resonate, resonance. The way sound travels through a drum.

Your hand feathers my pixie bangs. Over and over they lift and fall back to my forehead. It's a first memory, so old it comes from before memory, from the body. Always the feeling of being taken in, of arms wrapping around me, hugged to a warm chest.

I glide over Southern voices like soft, easy waves. I could rest in them all day. Floating, swelling, dropping, nothing too fast or hard.

Women's voices. Laughter.

10

NICKNAMES

The South is the land of the nickname, and people go by them as often as not. I grew up with an uncle I only ever knew as Rabbit; a woman who was a friend of May and Billy's went by Dunk; another relative whose last name was Thorn was called Aunt Sticker. A great-great grandmother who I never knew, Carrie Hawkins, was known to all as Ma Hawk. And from the tales about her and her sternness, her hawkish nickname was apt.

May's mother, Willie Mae Tennille, born in Georgia on October 20, 1894, was known as "Wea Wea." Someone's inability to pronounce the letter "L" in her name Willie turned into a permanent and widely used nickname.

I must tell you that it seems as though no one outside the South seems to be able to correctly pronounce Wea Wea despite my best lessons, and end up referring to her as "Wee Wee." But it goes like this: "Wi" as in "wick," and "We" as in "wee." Many people referred to her as Miss Willie and also as Mee Fitty, another nickname resulting from someone's difficulty saying Miss Willie.

Sixty-eight when I was born, Wea Wea was what people would call salt of the earth—sweet, do anything for you, with a simplicity and naive straightforwardness that often led to stories being told of her and some embarrassing situations—like when certain things went missing.

11

TELL ME A STORY

The first summer I date my now-husband, he begins his unwitting induction to The Stories, the ones that are always tumbling out. Sitting around the dinner table talking, one of us eventually nudges him. "Tell that story about...," asking him to recount something we've heard him tell about his days crewing on a large wind jamming ship or scuba diving or some other adventure.

In the beginning, he looks confused at these prompts and doesn't know what we're asking for. He doesn't think of his experiences in terms of stories, just things that happened to him or things he's done. After enough time around us, however, he starts to understand that he has stories too. Not only that, he learns what it means to tell one.

When I say "Tell me that story about [X]," there's a thing I'm hoping for, a way I want the telling to come out, what I'm expecting to hear.

I want the juicy details. I want a *story,* not a report. And for better or worse, I default to story. When someone asks, "Where did you get your dog?" a report would be "at the humane society."

But the *story* goes like this: It was December 27. The kids were at a sleepover and my husband and I decided to go BACK to the humane society to look at the puppies he and the kids had looked at the night before while they killed time before their movie started.

Because why not? What could possibly go wrong? What could possibly happen for us, people whose oldest dog of two had died a few months ago? People who had said to their kids, no, we're not getting a puppy, we still have a dog and we don't need a puppy right now. People who frequently had two dogs.

So we went in, and it was two days after Christmas, and they had tiny, adorable puppies.

And we found her. The one that wormed her way into our no-we-aren't-getting-a-puppy hearts. And her name was Sugarplum. When we went back to get her the next day, well, they had mistakenly given our Sugarplum to someone else. We were sad. And, yeah, pretty mad. But then we found another puppy and *she* became our Sugarplum. And there she was in our living room the next day when our kids came home from their sleep over, yipping and nipping and squealing.

And now we say we had visions of Sugarplum dancing in our heads.

That's a story, not a just-the-facts-ma'am-we-got-her-at-the-humane-society report.

I'll grant you that storytelling takes time, that you often have to settle in. That there are times when just-the-facts is called for.

But I want the stories, the way my family dished them up. I want you to paint a picture for me. I want to see the scene in my head. Because I'm curious. I'm curious about how you approach things, how you see the world, what you think about, how you make decisions, how you do (or don't) think things through.

I want to hear stories because I'm curious how people make

their way through this life. I want to hear the funny, the poignant, the misguided, the bittersweet, the real, the true.

True. With a little "t." Your truth, how you arrived there, how you walk through the world.

Joan Didion said, "We tell ourselves stories in order to live." I'm going to take it further than that and say we also need to tell our stories, not just to ourselves, but to others. And to hear stories told to us.

It's ancient, this storytelling. It's the original book and telegraph wire and email. It's where we started as a means of connection. It lives deep in our psyche.

12

THE ONE ABOUT THE UNDERPANTS

"Mom, tell me the underpants story again."

I'm sitting at her kitchen table. Or mine. Or anyplace really.

She laughs and then begins.

She tells me on Saturday mornings she, her brother Ricky, and their cousin Kathy would walk into town with Wea Wea to do errands. They'd go to Rose's 5 & 10 store where they'd spent the quarters Wea Wea gave them, mostly on gifts for her. Usually, mom says, they bought plates with pictures of Jesus painted on them that found their way to a special spot on Wea Wea's dining room wall.

One summer morning, dressed in a sundress with her pocketbook hooked over her arm, Wea Wea and the kids were on their Saturday walk through town and passed in front of Joiner's Market. Mr. Joiner and another man were sitting on the bench in front of the store, taking a break from work. Just as their little group passed in front of the bench, Wea Wea stumbled a bit. Mom looked down to see that Wea Wea's underpants had fallen from under her dress and were wrapped around her ankles. She was in the process of stepping out of them like nothing was happening. When Mom, Ricky and Kathy started saying, "Wea Wea! Wea Wea!" and pointing to the underwear, she said to them in a high pitched tone, "Tu-tu-tu-tu-tu! Come on children!" and continued to down the sidewalk, leaving her underwear where they fell.

13

SQUIRREL STEW—À LA B. L. CHANDLER

I now live in Boulder, Colorado, bastion of progressive politics, road cyclists, organic CSAs, farm to table meals, alternative healthcare and yoga. I know a few people who hunt, but mostly not, so when I announced recently at a small gathering that one of my favorite childhood foods was squirrel stew, every eyebrow at the table shot up in a collective WHAT? Suddenly I had a lot of questions to answer.

My best food memories come from the southern tables I sat at as a child—mostly the tables of my grandparents and others who fed me in Milledgeville. But especially the table of my Grandmother and Grandaddy (B.L.) Chandler. Both of them knew their way around the kitchen.

Their low, red-brick ranch style house sat under tall pines that soughed in the wind. Blue jays shrieked from the tops of the trees. Yellow and orange marigolds lined the flower beds around the back patio. Always yellow marigolds.

Steep brick stairs with no railing stepped up a half flight from the cool damp of the carport and into the kitchen. The stairs always terrified me with their sharp brick edges, their slickness, and the concrete that lay below. I never fell down them, despite much worry on my part and everyone else's that they would be my demise (that, and the constant worry that I would choke on a nut in Grandaddy's peanut brittle).

From the landing outside you stepped into the kitchen, where there was a small table on the right. Beyond it was a wide, c-shaped counter with a sink under the window and a gas range. Grandaddy sold propane for a living, and gas was the only way, as far as he was concerned, to cook, whether on the stove or grill.

The dining room was to the left, through a swinging door. In it sat a large, dark table that was always meticulously protected from water rings and scratches by coasters under sweating iced tea glasses and placemats under the plates. Against the wall stood a large chest of drawers, also made of dark wood, in an Empire style, heavy with broad, curled feet and an oval mirror hanging above it. A large, parlor-size opening connected this room with the formal living room. A jar of candy always sat on the coffee table in this living room and in the den—full of peppermints, butterscotch, and caramel squares. The butterscotch was my favorite. That and the few chocolate caramels that always came in the bag of regular ones. I'd dig to the bottom of the candy jar in search of the chocolate ones.

This room and table was the place for all family meals, including my all-time favorite (this recipe had, of course, been type written on one of Grandaddy Chandler's typewriters):

"Squirrel Stew—[A recipe]A la B. L. Chandler"

"Needed: Squirrel"

That was easy. We'd gather for a holiday and Granddaddy, my dad, my uncle Ray, and I would go out hunting. I was never excluded from these outings. It was a special quality of my dad's that he never told me I couldn't do things because I was a girl. He taught me to shoot his .22 rifle, use tools, swim, play soccer and basketball. In fact, none of those Georgia boys gave any indication that my being along on the hunt was unusual or bothersome.

I loved hunting with them, and was fascinated with the process of gutting and skinning the animals. Seeing the internal organs, opening the stomach to see if we could tell what the animal had eaten recently, looking at their little hearts. In fact, my dad told me recently I should have this bumper sticker for my car: "I love sunsets, beach walks, and poking dead things with a stick."

"Also needed: one pressure cooker, apple vinegar, celery, raw onion, garlic, pack of Lipton's dry onion soup mix, crushed red pepper, and grits + some bacon grease or 4 slices of bacon."

" ...saturate a cloth or something with vinegar and daub both sides with same. Let alone for about 45 minutes and then salt & pepper on both sides. Give this about 30 minutes to grab hold."

We'd gut and skin the squirrels, then put them into the pressure cooker, whole, heads and all, thus producing my Aunt Sally's favorite part of this meal, her own personal delicacy of squirrel brains. Let me say that I never went so far as to eat the brains. But I waited with fascination to see her eat them.

"Put about two tablespoons of bacon fat in or about four slices of bacon in bottom of cooker. Put in meat (do not fill cooker over 1/2 full). Add the things mentioned in part 1. According to the amount of meat being cooked, I usually use a medium to large raw onion, garlic, etc. Also a large stick of celery-cut up. Take it easy on the crushed red pepper. However, you eat the Mexican food, so just do as you wish on this." This last sentence a note to my father who was living in Texas and a fan of spicy Mexican food.

I now use a pressure cooker to cook many things, but I spent years terrified of them. Grandmother and Grandaddy used one frequently, but a famous family story of Grandaddy trying to take a short cut, removing the lid from the cooker too soon and blowing turtle soup all over the kitchen, made me wary.

"Let the pressure (after just about covering meat with water) get up to steam, ...cook for about 40 minutes and then let pressure go down. Remove meat, make a flour and water thickener, and thicken the gravy. I usually make the flour & water mix in a bowl and use an egg beater to mix. Then after I have slowly added to the gravy (have it at a slow boil) I use the egg beater to see that everything is proper as to any lumps of flour."

"You should have put the grits on about 15 minutes ago. If you did so, you are now ready to eat."

Needless to say, squirrel stew is served over grits.

Other game graced this table too—venison stew (same as squirrel stew, just substitute venison), Brunswick stew made with venison, duck, rabbit.

Now when I taste some of this game or other Southern foods like cornbread, turnip greens, venison, "sweet tea" (sweetened iced tea), pork rinds, or Coca-Cola—I'm immediately plunged back to these beloved tables.

Now, if I can just get my hands on a squirrel...

14

PORK RINDS & KOMBUCHA

My New England born, bred and life-long East Coaster mother-in-law stood in front of my pantry this morning and looked up. Spying the very large tub of pork rinds on the top shelf, she asked, "Who eats pork rinds?"

"I do," I said. "I do."

My favorite afternoon snack is pork rinds and locally brewed kombucha.

Boulder meets Milledgeville.

15

TALKING OUT LOUD

May and I were in Daytona, out for an afternoon of shopping, standing outside a clothing store and looking at the window display.

She was talking, but quietly, and I didn't catch what she said.

"I'm sorry—what? I didn't hear you."

"Oh—that's okay, Shug. I was just talking out loud."

She meant she was talking to herself.

I realize I talk out loud a lot.

16

BUD

Uncle Bud, that's what a lot of people called him. I just called him Bud. He was my great-grandfather, May's daddy, Wea Wea's husband. Born in 1898 and sixty-four years old when I was born, he was a thin man, wiry in the way of people who are always moving or fidgeting. Arms and legs that dangled off his torso. He had a handsome face, dimpled and angular with a devilish smile. He had a ready laugh and a twinkle in his eye.

I've seen photos of him as a young man dressed in a dark suit, black hat tipped rakishly on his head, foot propped on the chrome bumper of a fat, shiny black car. I remember him when he was older, always casually dressed in work pants or chinos and short sleeve shirts that allowed me to see the tattoo of a hula girl on the inside of his forearm—the one he could make dance by flexing and relaxing the muscle in his arm.

Bud was a mover and shaker in Milledgeville, an entrepreneur before the concept existed. At various times he owned a Chinese restaurant, a taxi cab company, a liquor store, and a beauty salon. The taxi cab company and the liquor store he also owned often joined forces to make deliveries.

At one time, he owned an auto garage with a mechanic that did repairs and two fuel tanks out front to sell gas. Everyone referred to it as "The Place." The garage had lots of room in it and Bud used part of it to store and resell furniture he bought from people and from the old Baldwin Hotel across the street.

Besides the cab company, Bud had a bus charter company and owned the first bus line from Milledgeville to Macon. The buses were all housed at The Place.

Bud developed and patented one of the first corn muffin mixes, called "Muffette." He had an old bus he converted to be a demonstration bus. One of his sons, Red (because of his red hair), drove around Georgia showing people how to use the mix.

May says Bud never met a stranger. She recalls their lunch and dinner table always having at least one person dining at it who Bud had brought home—either old or new-found friends.

People knew he was the person to call to get bailed out of jail so the phone rang night and day. Off he'd go to bail them out, often bringing them home for a meal. When Bud died, our family found a dresser drawer inches deep with little scraps of paper full of hand-written IOUs from a lifetime of people he'd helped.

When I was a child, Wea Wea and Bud still owned The Market Basket, a little grocery, bait and tackle, and liquor store outside of town. I remember going out to the store, a little white clapboard building with big silver coolers out front. I'd look inside at the bait worms wriggling round inside.

Wea Wea and Bud lived in a house about a block outside of downtown, not far from the Georgia Military College and across from the big brown Episcopal Church and its wide pine tree covered lawn. The house was a two-story light-yellow clapboard with a daylight basement that opened to the back. During the time I knew them, they lived downstairs in the basement area where they had a sitting room, combined dining/kitchen area, a single bedroom, bathroom, and a formal living room I'm not sure anyone ever went into. I certainly never did. The rooms upstairs in the house were rented out to tenants.

I remember Bud as a joker, someone with a big grin and a ready laugh. He did once bring a live baby alligator home from Florida as a present to my mom and her brother when they were kids. He put it into the bathtub at May's house but she was having none of it and made him take it with him when he left.

I was fascinated with his tattoo and wanted to see her dance, but was too shy with him to ask very often. I did, however, often ask him to make the sound of a "nanny goat" for me, an imitation he did well. He'd make the noise a few times, pat my arm or pinch my cheek and flash his dimpled smile.

Sometimes my mom would tell Bud she wanted to bring a friend over to introduce to him. He'd say to her, "Oh, that's alright honey, I got enough friends already." I'm not sure he ever did much he didn't want to do.

17

SINKER

Neither Wea Wea or Bud could swim but they both LOVED fishing and being out on the water. Sometimes from the shore at local ponds, sometimes at bigger lakes near home or in Florida from their fishing boat.

When May was a child, it was common in the summer for the family to go to a local pond to picnic and swim. The four kids—Bubba, Red (more nicknames!), May, and Betty—would be dressed up in their Sunday finery. The ladies would wear summer dresses and hats, the men their fine suits.

They'd take a huge picnic—fried chicken, potato salad, deviled eggs, pimento cheese sandwiches, sweet tea—all the things that make a good southern lunch. It would be packed into a large basket along with a blanket to sit on.

Bud had a large touring car. Everyone would pile in and off they'd go. When they got to the pond, they would change out of their fancy clothes into their swimming costumes.

Wea Wea would wade out into the water. Despite being unable to swim, she wasn't afraid. But everyone says that if she got deeper than her waist, somehow, she'd tip over, head down, feet up, and sink. May told me that one of the kids was always assigned to her while swimming and was responsible for righting her if she listed.

18

A LITTLE SOMETHING TO REMEMBER
ME BY

"May, that table covering is pretty," I say to her.

The white round tablecloth hangs to the floor and has a ruffle around the edge. Sitting on it is a silver framed photo of my hugely blue-eyed cousin as an infant, a delicate box, decoupaged with black and gilt, and a low lamp.

"Oh, Shug!" she laughs. "That thing is so old! Do you know what it started out as?"

"No—tell me!"

"It used to be a dress—one your sweet little mama wore on a float in a parade after she won the Miss Milledgeville pageant."

My mother, Miss Milledgeville? To hear about this seems so incongruous to me. When I was a child, we had Ms. Magazine in our house, beauty pageants were regarded as silly at best and demeaning to women at worst. By the time I hear this story about my mom, we're both adults and we have "come a long way, baby."

But, in her beauty queen days, May tells me, Mom needed a white dress to wear to an event in the pageant and also on the float in the parade. That May would sew it for her was never in question. May went to the fabric store to buy white organdy. Organdy is a fine, light, translucent fabric that is often stiffened and used for women's clothing. In other words, it's good for making fluff.

"The organdy at the store wasn't good quality, you know?" May says. "Stiff, and too coarse. Well, I had some organdy curtains with eyelet on the hem hanging in the middle bedroom. The fabric was nice—soft and silky. I took them down, stood Suzanne up and sewed the dress onto her. I never knew if it would stay up. It was strapless. But it did. I think we stuffed the bosom with socks or tissue."

Mom says lots of boys lusted after what was in the bust of her dress. Little did they know they were lusting after balled up tissues.

At some point, May took the dress apart and made the cloth for the table that now sat beside her bed.

"It's right pretty, isn't it?" she asks. "I lacked one inch of eyelet around the hem so I just turn that around to the back and nobody notices."

Mom says this is the reason she could never learn how to sew from May. The first thing May would do, if she even bought a pattern in the first place, was to throw the directions away.

I'm at her house with her one night when I'm about eight or nine. She's making a red jacket with slim lapels that comes just to her waist. It's late at night as usual because who sews during the day? Not us night owls. Just about finished, all she needs to do is sew the sleeves in. She does this (directions long gone, of course), puts the garment on a hanger, and holds it up for me to see.

Howls. We're both screaming with laughter and trying not to wake Billy. She has sewn the sleeves in backwards and they stick out towards the back of the jacket like wings. We both think it looks like a red chicken on a hanger.

It's during some other sewing session with me as helper that May sets up the ironing board to press seams or get the wrinkles out of the fabric she's about to cut. When she sews, she sets up the machine on the long table that divides the kitchen from the den. The ironing board sits by the table, just in front of the stove. The entire room is carpeted in a short-weave, dark green carpet.

It's my job to iron. I spread the fabric out on the silver ironing board cover and stand the iron on its end while it warms up.

Once the iron is hot, I start pushing the smooth hot metal over the fabric, then setting the iron back on its end while adjusting the cloth so I can press all of the sections. My right elbow bumps the iron, and off it flies onto the floor, landing, just like buttered toast, hot side down. In the seconds it takes to snatch the iron from the floor, a perfect black iron base singes onto the carpet, complete with the little holes where the steam comes out.

I am horrified and start to cry. Look what I've just done! Now there is an unmistakable and not subtle burn mark right in front of her stove and right behind Billy's chair at the table. She would never yell at me, I know that. But surely she'll be disappointed or chagrined or frustrated. Even I can see what it will take to fix something like this.

She grabs me and hugs me. "Oh, Shug," she says. "Don't you worry, you sweet thing you. Every time I see that mark, I'll think of you."

That mark stayed there for another forty years until she sold that house and moved into an apartment.

These are the things that formed me. Watching her improvise, create, make mistakes, laugh and move on. That approach to life, the laughter. Being hugged when I made a mistake instead of being taken to task. The giant blemish I had just made on her floor transformed instantly into something to cherish. It could so easily have gone the other way. Punishment, or simmering disappointment. Instead: mistake, laughter, move on.

I see now the blessing of this thread that moved through my upbringing: being viewed as good, worthy. She and Billy passed it on to my mom and her brother, and on to me. And I hope I've done the same for my children.

19

A GIFT

Shortly after my fifty-ninth birthday, a small cardboard box with Mom's return address and handwriting on the label turns up on my porch. I bring it inside and use the serrated steak knife that doubles as a package opener to cut the clear tape holding it closed.

Inside is a gold fine-mesh drawstring bag. Dangling from the bottom are teal and purple beads secured with gold braided thread. The bag is a beautiful gift itself. White peeks through the mesh. Picking it up, I feel the crinkle of tissue paper surrounding something flat and stiff. As I unwrap the paper, a thin, solid silver bracelet falls onto my kitchen countertop. I immediately recognized it as the bracelet May wore for as long as I can remember. Tears prick my eyes.

I gasp when I put the bracelet around my wrist. Despite having spent my life playing in May's jewelry, putting this bracelet on my arm is something I've never done. This ring of silver spent forty or fifty years on May's wrist, accompanying her everywhere she went, for everything she did, and for everything we did together. A witness to it all.

A much smaller version of the same bracelet is tucked into

my jewelry box, one that fit my childhood arm. May and Billy bought it for me on one of our Williamsburg trips. Wearing my own matching bracelet as a child made me feel special and connected to her, to them. It reminded me of our travels, of standing beside May as the jewelry maker hammered and shaped the shiny metal, stamped it inside with his mark, polished it, and placed it on my wrist. When it got too small, I wondered if someday I'd pass it on to a child of my own.

Now I wear May's bracelet every day. My heart leaps when it peeks out from beneath my sleeve. I rest my fingers on it for a moment before I put it into my jewelry dish at night. Sometimes, while it's on my arm, I circle my fingers around it for a moment and breathe. It's a wonder to me that it still exists and that now it lives with me. A tiny touchstone on my body reminding me of May's hugs, her unconditional love, her belief in my perfection just because I existed.

When I pluck it out of the small ceramic dish where it lives to put it on my arm, I say, talking to her: "Come on. You're coming with me."

20

THE BRACELET SPEAKS

Lord, May loved that child. And I don't mean she grew to love her. No, she started adoring her the moment she knew she existed. Sure, she was all nervous for about five minutes when she found out that child's mama was pregnant with Chris. Seventeen, just graduated from high school and on her way to college.

May knew it wouldn't be easy—two young people going to college and raising a baby. I sat there on her arm and watched it all. The glum, shocked faces. No one knowing what to do while knowing there was only one choice in Georgia in 1961. That these two young people, the child's mama and daddy, would get married and make the best of it.

But Miss May, she did what she usually did. She took it in. She had a moment of panic and then she marched ahead, never looking back. People have this idea of Southern women, especially of that time, as being meek and weak, but I'd say they confuse manners with what's really on the inside. There's a reason for the term "steel magnolia."

That baby's mama and daddy went and got married. By the

time they returned, Miss May had moved ahead. Nothing to do but plan for the arrival of that grandbaby.

The birth wasn't easy for mother or baby, and that baby came so early. And the labor was so terribly long. May was worried to death along with Billy and the Chandler grandparents. They spent three days pacing the hallway in shifts.

When that doctor finally came out and said, "You have a baby girl!" May and Grandaddy Chandler grabbed each other's hands and skipped around in a circle. They did that joyful dance and never looked back.

21

DRESSED

May was petite, a little over five feet tall and always wearing something crisp and colorful. When I see her in my mind's eye now, it's in a pair of white capri pants or a white skirt, a top in a bright yellow or orange, big florals, or the jewel colors. She was spunky and a force to be reckoned with in her own sweet southern way—sweet on top but you shouldn't get on her wrong side. She'd never diss you directly, but you'd know. Little southern ladies have a way of putting you into your place without ever saying a direct word. Legion in the South is the phrase, "Why, bless your heart!," which, based on inflection, can either express empathy or a cold, teeth-clenched dismissal.

In the morning, part of the dressing ritual was putting on her makeup in her small bathroom off her bedroom. The toilet and sink sat next to one another. Across from them was a narrow wooden table with thin legs and one drawer sitting under a window that looked out onto the front porch and yard.

"I have to put on my face," she'd say. For her generation of women in the South, it was unquestioned that you would wear foundation, face powder, blush (or as she called it, rouge), mascara, perhaps eyeliner, eyeshadow, and lipstick.

I would perch on the toilet lid and watch while she performed her makeup ritual, scents filling my nose—the light, fresh smell of face powder, the sweet waxiness of lipstick, the way the hairspray felt fizzy and tickly, like carbonation, in my nose. Pots and tubes and bottles of potions were taken from drawers and cabinets, lids scudding on and off, contents shaken and dabbed.

Hair had to be "done," which could include rollers, a hairdryer, a comb for teasing and adding height, a pick for further fluffing, possibly a curling iron. And, of course, no 'do was complete without hair spray.

And then there was getting dressed. No one dashed into town in their sweatpants (highly improper!) and yoga pants certainly were not a thing. No—I knew from watching that, though it was okay to be dressed casually, it was important to be "dressed" for town. Dressed included all of it. Makeup, hair, and clothes in a casual but put-together style.

Ultimately I would reject most of those things except a touch of blush and subtle lip color on my palest days. My curly hair has relieved me of doing much except wash and wear.

Don't get me wrong, I love a cute outfit. I often dressed up in May's clothes, picking bright scarves to fling around my neck, clip on earrings, tinkling bracelets, flowing patterned skirts and high heels. I played in her makeup, putting on eyeshadow and lipstick.

Her closet was full of clothes and shoes—some high heels but mostly casual shoes. And a good number of them because she rarely saw a pair of shoes she didn't like. Since she was small, it didn't take long for her clothes and shoes to almost fit me by the time I was ten or twelve. I could imagine my grown-up self as I put together dress-up outfits from her closet. Even though I'm not much of a shopper, I enjoy shopping with my mom, close girlfriends, and with May when she was alive. She was generous and usually sprung to buy something for me, even once I was a teenager and had my own money to buy things.

We'd come home with our purchases and she'd have me do a fashion show for her and Billy. I'd take everything out of the shopping bags and lay the clothes on her bed. Then I'd put them on, walk down the hallway to the living room where they'd sit waiting for me. I'd stand, then turn around so they could see the front and back.

"That looks just *precious* on you!," she'd say to me.

"Perfect, dahlin'," Billy would tell me.

May always carried a "pocketbook." I'm sure she used some that were of the more standard variety but the two I remember were both baskets. One was large and woven with wide flat strips like a picnic basket. It had a flat wooden lid painted with orange and yellow flowers and a flat handle that looped over the top. The other one, much smaller, was woven from a thin rattan and had a faux scrimshaw carving of an old sailing ship on the top.

In her bag was always gum, either Juicy Fruit or cinnamon, lipstick, a compact with face power for quick touch-ups, and a hair pick with narrow metal teeth for fluffing her hair. She'd rummage around in it looking for car keys or the powder compact so she could check her lipstick in the mirror or do a quick dab on nose and cheeks before getting out of the car.

May was an "everything away" housekeeper. Visible surfaces were clutter free and neat. Heaven help you if you looked in a drawer. She had long established a habit of tidying as she went. When leaving home, she would start at the back of the house in her bedroom and bathroom and gather items that needed to be put away. She'd pick them up, put them into her large pocketbook and deliver them to the room where they belonged as she made her way to the front of the house.

One day we drove into town, one of her big basket purses sitting on the front seat between us. In Joiner's Market she picked up a few items needed for dinner, something from the butcher counter, rolls, a few vegetables in the produce aisle. I followed her to the front of the small narrow store where she placed the items on one of the checkout belts and they ran forward towards the clerk.

"Hello, Miz Donnelly! How're you doin' today?" he said to her.

"Oh, just fine! How about you?"

"Fine, just fine!" He told her the total for the groceries. She reached into her purse to dig for her wallet. The next thing I knew, she was laughing so hard she could hardly talk. Finally, she pulled a half-full glass of water from her bag and held it up. I knew she'd picked it up somewhere along her home-tidying route and failed to drop it off in the kitchen.

"You'll never believe what I just did . . . ," she said to the clerk as she pulled the glass from her bag.

22

NO QUESTIONS ASKED

"**M**om. Can you come?" My voice was whispered, low, monotone.

I am in junior high school. My friend Carol and I have *finally* been invited to a party by a *cool* girl. We are so excited we spend way too much time deciding what to wear, trying to make our desperate attempts at casual and cool look tossed off and easy, belied by the piles of discarded outfits flung onto the bedroom floor. All this angst for the just-right combination of jeans and a t-shirt.

We had answered the requisite questions—whose house? Diane. Would her parents be home? Yes. Who else would be there? Kids from school.

As my mom drives us the twenty minutes to Diane's house, Carol and I sit in the back seat together, smiling at one another as we anticipate our entrée into the popular crowd. I imagine a shining future in front of me where the blond quarterback I have a mad crush on knows my name, sends me a carnation with x's and o's on Valentine's Day, and I am more than casual friends with some of the girls who wear their cheerleading outfits to school on game days.

Mom drops us off in front of the party house, then drives back toward home to finish preparing for the dinner guests she and my stepdad are expecting. It's around 7 pm, already dark outside. The porch light is on at Diane's house. Dim light shines from behind closed curtains. Our sneakered feet slap the cold sidewalk as we make our way to the front door and into the house.

It takes less than five minutes inside to see that things are less than good and to have any sense of my own coolness evaporate. Kids are already visibly, scarily drunk. The lights are low. A couple on the couch is intertwined in a way that makes me both want to stare and turn away. Clearly there are no adults here and we are way out of our league.

We don't have to talk—my eyes met Carol's in instant agreement. We both want out. Now. So much for my visions of utter coolness and being part of the popular crowd. If this is it, I don't want it.

But I'm not *so* uncool that I want to get caught calling my mom. There is a phone hanging on the wall of the kitchen, the handset attached by a long coiled cord. Miraculously the kitchen is empty. In a rush, I dial home.

"Mom, can you come?" No "Hi, Mom, it's me." No explanation of the situation, just a rushed and desperate question.

She had always said, "I'll come get you, no questions asked."

She is true to her word.

"Yes," she says, and hangs up. She must have heard from my voice, the flatness of it, the whisper, the rush, that it was no time for questions.

Carol and I sneak out the front door, walk a few houses down and sit on the curb under a street light to wait for Mom— who has had to abandon her guests—to come get us.

She came to us with the same fierceness of love and

protection May and Billy gave when my mom had called and said, "Can you come?"

23

FAMILY TRADITION

One summer when I am eight or so, after Mom and Dad and I have moved to Texas, I go to Milledgeville to stay with May for a few weeks, as I often do. May works in the mornings at the library at Georgia Military School, which is right downtown. I go to work with her and play librarian—take notes on a steno pad, shelve books, neaten stacks of magazines, pretend to type official forms.

I am charmed by the manners of the cadets and officers who come into the library. The boys only mildly disturb the heavy hush when they walk in. As they push open the big wooden doors, sunlight slants in behind them and dust motes float and dance. They speak quietly and call her Miz Donnelly. They say "please" and "thank you." "Yes, ma'am" and "no ma'am." In here, it smells the way old libraries smell—of cold marble, ancient paper, binding glue, and dust.

May and Billy have a new station wagon. It has wood-grained paneling and a new-fangled tailgate and back window that, respectively, slide down into the floor of the car and up into the roof. We finish work at noon. Today, just as we are leaving, Billy calls to say May's new bicycle has arrived at the

Western Auto Store, where he works. The store is just across the street and a wide lawn from the library. He's going to bring the bike right over.

She puts him off. There's an errand she wants to run first. But he insists.

"Oh, Billy!" she says with a sigh, punctuating it with the barest suggestion of a foot stomp, a tight pinching of her lips. As usual, and over his objections, she is going to do it her way. So we run out and hop into the car, intending to do the errand anyway and be back by the time he gets out the door to roll the bike over.

I climb in across the driver's side and sit up on her purse, the big shellacked basket with the wooden lid painted with the bright orange and yellow flowers on the top. It's a perfect perch for me; I can see over the dashboard. She slides in next to me, closes the door, rolls down the windows, puts the car in reverse and WHAM! She backs into *the* largest tree on the entire campus. I fly off the purse from the jolt and look over at her to see her wig has flopped off into her lap. She grabs it and pulls it back on as I collect the contents of her pocketbook.

Hysterical with laughter, we get out to assess the damage. *Big* dent right in the middle of the shiny silver bumper, a nice impression of the tree. To make things worse, the tailgate won't push down into the floor of the car as it should. Through the pines across the grassy lawn, here comes Billy pushing the pink bike towards us, the glittery handlebar tassels shimmering and swaying.

This isn't the first time she's backed into a tree. A pesky one near the edge of their driveway has already caused problems. Right now, it is clear to both of us the only solution is to lie. It is a wordless, immediate decision made with one glance at each other.

"I'll lean on the dent."

"Okay," she replies, "I'll get him to put the bike in through the window."

As Billy approaches with the bike, we try to look casual while avoiding looking at one another. Eye contact is deadly and will make us laugh.

"Here," she says to him, reaching for the bicycle. "Just lift it right through the window. I'll help you." This is a tiny woman who couldn't begin to lift a heavy and awkward bike into the back of a car through a window. It's bound to seem odd.

"No! Just put the tailgate down!" he tells her.

"Just put it through the window!"

Around they go.

I'm not sure if it's her strange behavior or the fact her wig is on sideways that tips him off that something isn't right.

"May! What is the *matter* with you?!"

She motions for me to move. Stepping aside, I reveal the dent. We point to the offending tree. The *really* big one. You can't miss it. Even when you're backing up.

Recently I pulled out of my driveway to discover I had a flat tire. Instead of trying to do a three-point turn in the road, I backed into the driveway. And hit a pine tree. Now, not only did I have a flat, I also had a busted tail light and a nice scrape down the side of my car.

Oh well. Sometimes you can't avoid family tradition.

24

WHAT TREE?

May's neighbor, B., called May one day in a flutter. She'd been asked to go to Milledgeville's small airport to pick up Representative Carl Vinson, who didn't drive, and take him to a local event. It was sometime in the late 1950's. Rep. Vinson was returning to Milledgeville from Washington, DC on campaign business.

A Milledgeville native, Vinson represented Georgia in the U.S. House of Representatives from 1914-1965. Close friends with Bud and Grandaddy Chandler, many in my family simply knew him as "Uncle Carl" instead of Representative Vinson. But he was highly respected and treated so when he returned to his hometown.

"Please, May. Come with me! I don't want to go by myself," B. said.

"B, I haven't taken a shower yet. I'm not even dressed."

"May, pretty please!"

"Okay—I'll be there in 10 minutes."

May dashed around doing three things at once, dressing, fixing her hair, and putting on her makeup. After one last check in the mirror, she grabbed her pocketbook, rustled around inside it to make sure she had her keys, and dashed out the front door. She jumped into the driver's seat and put the car in reverse. Foot hard on the accelerator, she went fast up the long narrow driveway towards the street. She'd make it in time.

But there was just the problem of that big pine tree close to the side of the drive...

Wham!

What was THAT? She looked out to see the tree, the thick, very tall tree now stretched out across the lawn.

"Oh gawd!" A clench of her teeth, a little fist tapping the steering wheel. No time to spare, she left it there to be dealt with later. Before Billy got home.

When she got home, the tree still lay there. Somehow she got it out of the yard, though exactly how is disputed. One version goes that my uncle Ricky, still in high school at the time, had come home from school and became her unwitting accomplice. With his help, the tree was cut in half? Had some branches sawed off? Was dragged to the back of the house? Moved *somewhere* besides flopped across the lawn until she could have it hauled off the next day.

It was dark when Billy got home. But not dark enough that he didn't notice the big tree missing.

"May! Where'd the tree go?"

"Tree? What tree?"

She would not admit to knowing anything about a tree. As the story goes, Billy shrugged his shoulders, shook his head and sighed. Despite having disposed of the "body," there was still an unmistakable dent in the bumper.

Billy handled the household finances and most things

administrative so May had no experience in these areas. But he was miffed and insisted she deal with the auto insurance. In answer to the question on the insurance form, "In what direction were you traveling?," she answered "Backwards, in an easterly direction."

25

RAIN STOP!

May, Billy and I are riding along the highway on one of our journeys, ones we take in the summer when I spend several weeks with them. We're always going somewhere—to Macon, Florida, Warm Springs or Eagle Rock. It is with them that I learned to love a road trip.

When we're in Daytona Beach, we take rides down A-1-A past the tall hotels, the older, smaller motels with their neon vacancy signs squeezed in between. At my request, we stop at touristy shell shops where I pick up and turn over the exotic shells displayed in baskets—small ones with bright colors, brown ones with white spots, nautilus shells cut in half, revealing the interior swirls. We laugh at the coconut shells cut in half and connected to fashion bikini tops. I stare at the captive hermit crabs waiting to be sold and dragged back to some northern climate, where they'll likely be forgotten and die.

We ride along the road, me perched on the front seat, content to be right there with them, Billy driving, May sitting on the backseat. Billy keeps a packet of Red Man chewing tobacco in the pocket of the driver's side door. The packet rustles as he takes it from the pocket in the door and places it on the seat between his knees. The inner foil shines silver, the outside dark green with RED MAN in red writing, the image of a Native American man in a feathered headdress in a white circle. When the pouch opens, the acrid scent of tobacco drifts into the car. He places a little wad in his cheek, rolls the top closed again and tucks it back into the door.

Of course, the trip hasn't truly gotten started until we crack open the Cokes and crackers. Sometimes this requires a stop at a filling station to buy them. Sometimes May has a small cooler already filled with drinks and snacks.

May often writes postcards and paints her nails while we drive.

How she managed this, I still can't understand. I can barely paint my nails sitting still on my bathroom floor. The ting, ting, ting of the little metal ball shaking in a bottle of nail polish remains one of my favorite sounds. It is the sound of May and of a road trip.

Similarly, the tangy, sweet smell of Jergens Hand Lotion reminds me of May and these trips. She keeps a bottle in the door or middle console and offers it around each time she uses it on her hands.

May also often reads cookbooks while we drive. She collects recipes she finds in papers and magazines or from people we meet. She writes these in the back of the cookbook she's reading. Sometimes she cooks some of the recipes but I learn over the years it's more of an exercise in collection. She is not a great cook. In fact, she often tosses burned food off the back stoop into the back yard. An early form of composting, I suppose. Wea Wea, her mother, was a terrible cook, having never learned the skill well either. My mom says she dreaded having Sunday dinner at Wea Wea's house because, though she loved being with them, the food was burned, dry, and bland, and the gravy lumpy.

May loves music, so the radio plays at her request. "Billy, turn it up," she asks. She turns to me: "Don't you just love this one, Shug?" Stevie Wonder, Elton John, soft jazz, classic rock. Her musical tastes are as contemporary as mine. I'm happy to stare out the window at the passing scenery or on long trips, bury my nose in a book.

Billy's nature is quiet, reserved. He is a small man, a few inches over five feet tall and compact, stocky. He has the same dark brown eyes as my mother, a fine delicate nose, and dark, wavy hair. Because he is so quiet, I listen when he has something to say.

He is a lover of history of all sorts, so our trips often take us to places of historical significance—Warm Springs, Georgia, sites of Indian mounds, Civil War battlefields. He quietly teaches me what he knows about wherever we are. We take a turn through the museum or interpretive areas. But it's never boring or too much. The sites are the destination, but it's all about the adventure, the journey, what we'll see and discover, the mystery of hitting the open road, never knowing exactly what we'll find, even if we've been there before.

Sometimes southern summer downpours blanket the car, blinding the driver and slowing traffic to a crawl or bringing it to a halt. When driving along in one of these rains, Billy says, "Times, times, American times, eighteen hundred and seventy-nine." Then he snaps his fingers and says, "Rain stop!"

The deafening beat of rain on the roof halts. Silence. The windshield clears. And then, just as suddenly—drum, drum, drum—blinding rain and the beat of heavy drops.

It took me years to figure out this trick required passing under an overpass that quickly shielded the car from the rain.

They were my haven, the place where I knew I was the

favorite, could do no wrong, beloved and adored beyond all else. Those arms have stretched out over my life to provide such a solid shelter of love. Always reaching out to snap and say, "Rain stop!"

26

THE ONE ABOUT WISHING

If you ever said, "Wea Wea, I wish . . . ," she'd look at you and say, in her sweet high-pitched voice, without a hint of meanness or snark, "Sugar, wish in one hand and tiddle in the other and see which one fills up faster."

(Tiddle means "pee" in Southernese.)

It seems like good advice.

Somehow I find her phrasing of it easier to take in than "stop complaining." More of a statement of reality than an admonishment, a way of saying it that makes me think instead of telling me what to do.

Whenever "I wish . . ." surfaces in my head, her voice saying this comes back to me and stops me in my tracks. And I'm better for it.

27

THE SOUTHERN CROSS

It's June 1978, and I've just finished my sophomore year in high school. My mom, stepdad and I have just moved from Richardson, Texas to Aspen, Colorado. Despite the fact I'm in the middle of my high school years, I readily gave my stamp of approval for this move, eager to leave behind a culture of big hair and makeup for a life more oriented to the outdoors, jeans, and flannel shirts. No blow dryer required. In this little town, I'm immediately at home.

This is the year our high school is hosting our first exchange student with the American Field Service. Now our community is eligible to send students abroad for the summer. My high school counselor asks me if I want to apply.

"I'm nervous," I tell Mom as I sit on the kitchen counter. "It will be REALLY far away."

More than nervous, I'm *scared*. My stomach flutters and my eyes sting, like I might cry.

I'm used to flying on my own to visit May and Billy, and my dad, who has been living in Massachusetts for a few years—but someone I know and love has always been on the other end. That's the thing I understand now, as an adult: I could flip through life like a trapeze artist flinging herself through the air. But I could also see the net below, which were the people I knew and trusted. They were *right there.* And I was certain they would catch me if I fell.

But in this young moment, I wonder if I have what it takes to do this. I'll be going off to some place unknown. Into the care of people unknown. A place far, far away where there won't be an opportunity to bail, to pick up the phone and whisper, "Mom, can you come?" And if I need a safety net, I'm not sure how strong it will be.

As we talk, I feel a shift in my body, a solidity forming. Even though I'm scared, I know I'll regret it if I don't give it a shot.

As I fill out my application and look ahead, I imagine being placed with a family in a European country like France or Spain. The most exotic my thinking gets is South America. Imagine my surprise when, in mid-May, I open a big bright white envelope and pull out sky blue pages telling me I've been matched with a family in... Johannesburg, South Africa?! Talk about *far.*

A month later, I'm on my way.

~

When I look up at the night sky in South Africa, even the stars are unfamiliar. Gone are the Big and Little Dipper and Orion's Belt, replaced by the Southern Cross. So far, so foreign, so *other.*

Food is different, door knobs are different. They drive on the other side of the road, which is panic-inducing even as a passenger. They call the trunk of the car a "boot" and the hood a "bonnet." They say "Shame!" as an expression of "too bad"or "that's so sad." And, of course, there is the vast matter of apartheid and the discomfort of being faced with signs in public places that still say, "Whites Only."

I have my moments of homesickness, but they don't last long.

When I get word of the death of both a high school friend and an aunt, within a few days of one another, my host mother, Penny, pats and rubs my back as I lay sobbing, curled up in a ball on her bed.

"There, there," she murmurs.

She stays there, solid and patient, until I have cried all my tears. She mothers me as tenderly as her own.

My host family ends up feeling like part of my long lost family on the other side of the world. We have the same set of daily concerns—food on the table, making friends, desires to connect and develop relationships. Desires for recognition, love, validation. The same urge to gather around food, talk, laugh, share, cry. They are loving people who open their arms and their hearts. Forty-three years later, we remain connected.

In my journal from that summer, besides recording what I was doing and seeing, I wrote frequently about how much I missed my family, friends, and Aspen. But it was missing born of gratitude. I recorded an appreciation for my sweet mountain town, a place I called my soul home, for the community we had built around us in one short year, gratefulness for friends far and wide, for my parents and extended family.

I made note of how I was building a family in South Africa —with my host mother and father, my host siblings, with their extended family and with friends at school. About conversations we had about education and politics, about family and happiness, about navigating life.

Without realizing it, I was weaving my own net, testing its strength and bounce. At some point, I had to let go, fly through the air alone for a few dizzying seconds, look for the new bar or set of arms, and grab hold again.

28

FOR THE BIRDS

There was a small stoop on the back of May and Billy's house, a concrete pad, maybe six feet by six feet, surrounded by a black iron railing. From it, a flight of stairs led down to the yard. This exit from the house was not used for coming and going. But it was frequently used by May to rid herself of food—stale bread, burned dinners, leftovers that wouldn't get eaten.

"I'm going to feed the birds," she'd announce as she made her way to the door and out onto the porch.

From there, she'd fling the food down into the yard and whatever lucky creature found it could have at it.

Cheese wafers or cheese straws are a Southern staple, practically a required food for any baby shower, cocktail party, or ladies' tea. Made mostly with flour, shredded cheese, and butter, the dough is thick, sticky, and challenging to work with —though there are strategies to make it easier—(as noted in the recipe below).

One day May was making cheese wafers. She was attempting to make the small biscuits by pushing the dough through an extruder onto the baking sheet. I don't know if this approach actually works for anyone, but it sure didn't work for her. The dough was too thick to push through the end of the tool, but she kept trying. Finally, the whole kit and caboodle gave up the ghost and the extruder burst apart and clattered onto the metal sheet in pieces.

She'd had enough.

"TIME TO FEED THE BIRDS!"

She marched over to the door with the bowl of dough and the pieces of the broken tool. She pitched it all out into the back yard, turned back around, shut the door behind her, and that was that. I'm not sure what offering she took with her to wherever she was going, but it wasn't cheese wafers.

Luckily, there are easier ways (recipe follows):

Cheese Wafers

> **Cheese Wafers**
> *(courtesy of Hardy Chandler, my stepmother)*
>
> *1 cup grated sharp or extra sharp cheese (4 oz.)*
> *1/2 cup Rice Krispies*
> *1 cup all purpose flour*
> *1 teaspoon salt*
> *1/8 teaspoon cayenne pepper*
> *1/2 cup butter*

- Use the food processor as much as possible. Grate cheese with small grate disc, set aside.
- Put flour, salt and cayenne pepper in processor bowl with blade attachment and pulse to blend.
- Slice butter into small pieces and add to flour mixture. Pulse until butter is pea-size. Add cheese to flour/butter mixture and pulse until it is blended.

- Put cheese and flour mixture in a large bowl and add Rice Krispies. Mix with hands until it can be formed into logs. Wrap each log in wax paper and chill in refrigerator until firm.
- Cut into 1/4 inch slices. Bake in 350 degree oven for 12 to 15 minutes until lightly browned. Let cool in pan for a short time before placing on cooling rack.

This should make about 4 dozen wafers.

*You can buy an 8 oz. block of cheese and double the recipe. Two recipes will fit in the processor at one time.

*Try to cut the slices a little larger than 1/4 inch, which seems to hold them together better.

*Sometimes the oven temperature needs to be a little higher (365) so they cook faster.

Or, as Grandmother Chandler did it:

- Mixed dry ingredients together.
- Using a pastry blender or two knives, worked the butter into the flour mixture until it looked like small peas.
- Grated a block of cheddar cheese and added correct amount to butter/flour mixture.
- Mixed together with hands.
- Rolled dough into walnut-size balls and placed on baking sheet at least an inch apart.
- Pressed each ball with a dinner fork.
- Baked until brown, using instructions above.

Cheers! And good luck! It's worth it.

29

THE THIRD PERSON

May and I leave her house and step out onto the concrete porch that's painted a deep maroon red. Tall thin pine trees dot the yard, but there aren't enough to make bona fide shade.

The short deep-green boxwood hedges that run along the porch emit a bitter but not unpleasant odor. Blue jays squawk overhead from high in the trees. A breeze moves the hot, wet air, swaying the branches and needles.

I smell the tang of pine and a waft of sweet gardenia so enticing I poke my nose right into the cream-colored blossom on the bush by the driveway and inhale. My hand reaches out for May's and is met with the warm, soft tenderness of her grip as our palms meet.

She climbs into the driver's seat. I plop onto the front seat beside her. We toss beach towels into the back. We are headed for the John Milledge motel, a small roadside lodging just outside the neighborhood and on the main road into town. Low, white, with blue doors and a neon "vacancy" sign, it has a pool out front surrounded by a gray metal chain link fence. This is where we are headed in the heat of this summer day.

May knows the motel's owner and has gotten permission for us to swim there. She drives us the short distance, parks, and we climb out, making our way through the swinging gate.

With scrapes and screeches, we pull two lounge chairs across the concrete toward one another, arrange the tilt of the backs to our liking, spread our towels over the stretchy plastic slats across the chairs and arrange ourselves face up, to bask in the sun.

May stretches out, re-adjusts her dark glasses. I do the same with my smaller pair. I'm nine, but I could be eleven, sixteen, forty. Once I'm older, I'll be the one driving her. Once I can drive, I'll be the one steering her and Billy across town, as well as across the country.

But it really doesn't matter the age of either of us. We're friends, side-kicks, and our respective ages are irrelevant. On this day, I hop into the pool, jump off the diving board, and turn flips in the water, constantly imploring her to "watch this." If she gets sick and tired of it, she gives no signs.

After enough of that, I climb out and take up my place beside her again. She passes me a *Good Housekeeping*, *Seventeen Magazine*, or *Vogue*. We point out good or bad outfits, haircuts and shoes to one another. "That would look adorable on you!" she says, pointing out a shirt while re-applying suntan lotion and passing the bottle to me. NOT the kind that protected anyone's skin from anything.

She's there for so many things, the big and the small, in person and long distance on the phone and a lifetime of handwritten letters. And she's there at the airport, the summer day I arrive home in Aspen, Colorado from my Vermont college on a tiny airplane, the one that just makes it in through the hole in the clouds during the June 2 blizzard. And Mom, of course, she is there too, waiting for me.

But someone else. Someone I hadn't expected. Him. He is there too.

I walk down the metal stairs from the airplane onto the snow splattered tarmac. It is cold—not like the 80 degrees I've just come from.

Mom and May are waving from inside, behind the floor-to-ceiling windows. I was expecting them. But a third person, a head taller than them both, stands behind them.

He is also waving. A flash of recognition somewhere inside my brain, but also disorientation. I can't quite place him. And yet... yes, I know that face.

The blue eyes. The fine aquiline nose. The pull of his shoulders, back and straight. The blondish-brown hair that curls as it gets longer. The curls my college girlfriend cuts for him. The haircuts I loved to grill her about. Because I have a crush on him.

I smile and wave. If I were a blusher, I'd be beet red. I have the fifty steps from outside to inside and the time it takes to pluck my bag from the baggage cart beside the airplane to arrange my thoughts, to calm my galloping heart, to stop smiling quite so stupidly, broadly, wildly. To figure out how to get my face under control.

Well, this complicates the summer.

I am planning to leave Aspen in a few weeks for a summer program in Colorado Springs at Colorado College, one I have chosen and one, until this very moment, I was excited about. But something is already pulling me towards him. Towards staying here for the summer.

Don't change your plans for a man, is what Mom would say. *You aren't even dating.* Wise words I already know I will ignore.

There's a tickle and pull in my chest. I sense the way this is going and I haven't even set foot in my own front door.

It is a foregone conclusion, and I am the goner.

30

BACK HOME

When we're in the car after Adam shows up at the airport upon my return from college, Mom asks me, "Did you know he was coming?"

"No. I mean, yes. I mean, I knew he was going to be here for the summer staying with B. But, no, I had no idea he'd be here today. I'm not even sure how he knew what time or what day I was getting here."

"He called me this morning to find out," she said. "He wanted to come meet you. He was pretty persistent. Was it okay that he came?"

"Yes, fine. Good."

May and Mom both stare at me for a beat longer than normal. Mom seems annoyed. I'm still smiling too widely. May squeezes my hand. I squeeze back.

Mom drives, May sits in the passenger seat and I sit in the back of our old Jeep with the dent in the hood as we drive up the valley toward home.

I relax into the joy and comfort of homecoming, of being taken in by two sets of arms that have received me all of my life. In a few hours the late-season snow will melt and summer will re-emerge. Aspen leaves shimmer in the breeze like jazz hands welcoming me home.

And now, dusted onto the top of that perfection is new love. I can feel it in my bones.

~

For the next few weeks, Adam and I spend as much time together as possible, then I leave for Colorado College as planned. May and Billy are still visiting, and drive me the several hours from Aspen to Colorado Springs. More accurately, as has long been our tradition, I drive and they accompany me.

They help me get settled into my dorm room, take me to the store for a few last-minute items. May, ever the decorator, finds me an adorable lamp with a checkered lamp shade that she adds to my room. They treat me to dinner, drive off to their hotel and return to Aspen the next day.

~

When I wake up the next morning and look around, I am not happy. I've come here sight unseen and I don't like it. I tell myself I don't like the setting, that I don't like it *here*. Where I've spent a sum total of about 23 hours.

~

I find the pay phone at the end of the dorm hallway.

"Mom, it's me. I don't want to stay here."

"Chris, you've made a commitment to this summer program. And you have been so excited about it. What's going on?"

"I just don't like it. I don't like it here. It's too hot and dry and dusty. It's ugly. Just bare red rocks everywhere. It's like a desert and there isn't anything green. I'm homesick. I want to come home."

"Is this about Adam?" she asks.

"No. I just want to come *home*. Can I talk to May?"

"Yes, here she is."

"May, I hate it here. I don't want to stay."

"Shug, don't you worry. You know how Billy and I love a road trip. We'll come get you."

31

HOW TO BUILD A SAND CASTLE

Daytona Beach is known to the world as a tacky, over-developed place where college kids go crazy over spring break. And it is that. But I see it with different eyes. For me, it's the place Wea Wea and Bud spent their vacations fishing, where my grandparents and parents and I vacationed as children.

It's the place we would arrive in the darkness after the drive from Georgia. I knew we were close when the scent of the air changed to salty, sandy, fishy. There was no going to bed without putting our feet into the sea. In the darkness, we'd go down to the ocean with flashlights, watch crabs run on the beach, and stand in the calf-deep surf squealing as large runs of small silver fish jumped and flew by, bumping our legs.

It's the place we drove back roads to go to restaurants for fried shrimp and hush puppies, through marshy land thick with squat live oak trees, moss hanging from the branches, a still blue heron balancing on one leg, bright white egrets perched on fallen logs. A place where dolphins glided by beyond the surf break, where pelicans floated silently overhead and crashed headlong into the ocean, fishing for their next meal.

It's where May and Billy would take me to the Hawaiian Inn to eat dinner and watch the hula show. I was so awed by the dancers, I could barely eat my beloved fried shrimp. The women moved so fluidly, like they were floating in water. The Hawaiian music, the language, the bare feet and swaying hips were so exotic and foreign and mysterious to me. Back in our room, I would stand on the bed and dance in the grass skirt May and Billy bought for me.

It's also the place May and I spent hours on the sand making drip castles. She taught me how and we constructed hundreds over the years. Position on the beach is important. Too far from the water and your moat will be dry—and water is essential. Too close and the water will seep in too fast, eating away at the moat walls, sheet by sheet of sand flaking off and sliding down until the castle's foundation is eaten away.

This is how you do it: dig a hole in the sand. The hole should fill slowly with water. Pile the excavated sand up into a cone near the hole. Now—dip your hand into the hole, scoop up the wet sand and let it drip down your finger into little round stone-like blobs.

Drip, drip, drip, controlling the flow for larger or smaller drops to cover your cone and then gradually build balconies, turrets, arches, bridges, flagpoles, spires and walls.

This works because the crystals that make up the sand are so fine it forms into neat gray spheres that stack one on top of the other. The sand is as fine as sugar. Mixed with the right amount of water, it flows easily along one downward-pointed finger. I learned over time to control the amount of sand and water to achieve drops large, medium or small depending on what I was building and the look I wanted to achieve.

Coquina shells, small fingernail shaped shells of pale purple, pink, yellow and orange, serve as flags, sentries, queens and kings on balconies. Finally, a castle stands complete, surrounded by a full moat, fortress walls, a bridge and a smooth sand yard.

Eventually the tide creeps in, tongues of water lapping ever closer, taking down the outer wall, over filling the moat. With the next slurp, the castle is surrounded, but still standing. The receding water pulls away the rest of the moat walls. The lower turrets topple, the moat caves, and now it looks like a lump of sand with spikes sticking out of the top. Tomorrow the building site will be smooth, no evidence of construction.

Every visit to the beach, even now at sixty years old, I build at least one. At first I feel ambivalent. I want to do it. It is my own tradition now—and a way to pull May back to me, to see the shape of her hands as she dripped sand, to hear her soft southern voice, to hear her laugh—but it's so messy. To do it right requires putting my bare legs on the sand and being on hands and knees, leaning over, digging, getting sandy and gritty. There comes a moment when I abandon myself to the grit, leaving behind adult considerations of staying clean. Once I commit, being a mess feels good. For now I am solely a castle builder, giving way to my imagination, May sitting beside me.

When I finish, I dedicate my creation to her by writing MAY in huge letters in the sand. I surround it with the outline of a heart.

32

THE LOW DOWN

I'm with May in Ormond Beach, FL at a condo right across the road from the beach where she spends a few months each spring. I am here to spend a week with her, just the two of us. I've been back home in Aspen working and waiting for Adam—the one who took my breath away at the airport—to finish his officer training with the Coast Guard.

That first morning, May is standing in front of the sliding glass door, pulling the long hanging slats of the shade to one side. Somehow she is up and moving before I am. She has on a bright floral bathing suit, her feet are bare, her toenails and fingernails painted a pearly pink, as always. Under one arm she clutches a *Ladies Home Journal* and a *People* magazine. A straw hat sits on her head and she already has her dark glasses on. A small folding chair is propped against the wall by the door. The sweet coconut scent of sunscreen is in the air. Once again, we're at the beach together, a happy place for both of us, but especially for her. She loves it best here.

"I'm ready to go!" she says, though that is fully evident.

"Oh, wow! You really are ready. Sorry to keep you waiting. You're quick this morning."

"I've already taken the trash out, avoided that neighbor lady three times, and folded a load of laundry! Nonny nonny nonny and a ha cha cha!" She does a little jig that includes some tap-dance-like steps and a hip wiggle. "I was a tap dancer when I was young, you know!" she reminds me. I laugh.

"Let's go to the beach first," I say.

We step out of the air-conditioned cool into the rising heat of a late-spring Florida morning. The air is moist. Seagulls squawk. The smell of the sea fills my nose, reminding me of all the times I've arrived here to step out of the car to this very same scent.

Holding our beach bags and carrying an umbrella, we walk across the thick, green grass, onto the pool deck, out the small wrought-iron gate and across the two-lane asphalt road to the wooden stairs that lead across and down the dunes to the beach.

Stopping at the top of the stairs on the narrow deck, May stops to look out over the sand and sea. The morning sun is still low in the sky. A few bright umbrellas dot the sand. Fishermen, barefooted with big bellies, stand with their feet in the shallow surf casting lines and watching bobbers.

The sea is flat and calm with small waves breaking close to the shore. The water rolls in, chasing sandpipers with their delicate, skittering steps up the sand. As the water recedes, they appear to chase it back out to the sea, just like it pursued them seconds ago. May does a little shiver of happiness.

"I just love those birds," she says.

To remind her of the beach, a carved trio of the gray and white sandpipers sits on a chest in her den at home.

Leaving our shoes on the deck at the top, we walk down the stairs across the wide flat expanse of sand and stop just above the sudden downslope near the tide line. This is where we unfold our beach chairs, ones that sit close to the sand, the ones May calls the "low down" chairs, good for sitting in the surf and letting the water rush in and over your feet—and the rest of you if you aren't careful. I twist the red umbrella into the sand between our chairs. We drop our bags full of towels, sunscreen, reading material and snacks, and both sit.

"Ahhh." We sigh as we sink into our chairs, the weight of our bodies pushing them down into the sand, lean back and stretch out our legs.

The waves roll in and out with a noise that sounds like shush, shush, shush. The sound is soothing. My body gets heavy in my chair. It reminds me of sitting on a warm lap, ear pressed to a chest, hearing the murmur of breathing.

We sit and gaze, taking it all in, not talking yet. Brown pelicans glide in a long line, out over the water, parallel to shore.

I've been thinking about what's next for me. And for me and Adam together. While I'm here with May, Adam will find out where his first duty station will be. We've already decided we want to be together, so I'm waiting with nervous and excited anticipation to find out where we'll be going.

I wonder how she'll respond. I don't think this news—my going to be where he is or our living together before we're married or even engaged—will faze her. But I'm not 100 percent sure. It's 1985; living together before marriage is becoming more common. But I'll be the first in my family. She has always supported my decisions, but this is the first one where I've stepped out there a bit, beyond what I'm sure is comfortable for her. I haven't pushed the bounds very much. Or ever.

I turn to her. "Adam is going to find out where his first assignment is going to be later this week. He wants me to come with him. So we'd live together."

"Oh, Shug! That's so exciting. Do you love him so much?" She grabs my hand and squeezes.

I take a big breath and let it out. I didn't realize I've been holding my breath and sitting with tight muscles until I feel it all relax in the embrace of her love and support once again.

"I do. I'm excited. But I'm a little nervous. Not about being with him. But I have no idea where we'll end up. Honestly, I don't even know what the possibilities are, but this is what I want to do."

She shifts in her chair, scooting her bottom back and sitting more upright then smiles. After a pause she says, "I remember when Billy and I got married. It was WWII and he was in the Army. We got married quickly because he was going overseas, but first we went to Ft. Lee, VA for his training. I had so much fun decorating our little apartment there."

We sit silently for a moment, her memories taking her back, me imagining her as a young bride. I push my feet forward and backward, digging a small hole in the sand, the grains rough against my feet. I close my eyes and lean my head back against my chair. A light breeze ruffles the edges of the umbrella, a loose hair tickles my nose. The waves have risen. Big rollers swell up, then sink down. Water crashes as waves finally get the best of themselves and tip over their own tops. In and out. In and out. Shush, shush, shush. I tip my head back into the chair, close my eyes and rest in the pause.

She laughs, and I know a story is coming. Her arm moves. The silver bangles around her wrist chime.

"I've probably told you this story before . . . ," she says. But it doesn't matter to me. I always want to hear the stories again.

"We had a tiny little apartment. The first thing I did, I painted the whole thing white. Bright white. It was so clean and fresh. Then I made these yellow and white gingham curtains for the windows. It was just adorable. I loved that little place."

She's staring out at the ocean as she talks, gaze unfocused, like she's seeing it all in her mind's eye.

"Did I tell you about the fur coat?"

She doesn't wait for me to answer. It's not really a question, just a lead-in to the story.

"Four of us Army wives, we went up to Washington, DC one day for lunch and shopping. Well, window shopping mostly. Or it was supposed to be!" A chuckle. "None of us had two pennies to rub together. We were all the wives of new officers. At first we just stood outside and looked at the furs in the window, but after a minute, we couldn't stand it and we went inside. And then, to make it worse, the sales woman came over with a beautiful coat just my size, really small. I put it on and felt so regal. I told myself I'd never find another one like it. So I bought it. It cost Billy's whole paycheck. I knew he'd be furious but that didn't stop me. He was fit to be tied!" she laughed.

" May! How could you DO that?!'" he demanded.

"But it was too late to do anything about it. He told me I'd have to keep the heat off in the apartment during the day to save money. And it was COLD!"

But he'd met his match.

"That was fine with me," she said.

She laughs, leaning forward and pinching the bridge of her nose.

"I just sat in the bed under the covers all day wearing my fur coat to stay warm, admiring my gingham curtains and talking to my girlfriends on the phone."

I'm not sure if Billy realized it at the time, but he was destined for a lifetime of this with her. I can't tell you how many times I heard this play out between them:

"May, is that a new outfit?" he'd ask.

"What? This old thing? I've had it for years."

It was brand new.

~

May's stories about money were funny—the ones I had heard and the ones I witnessed—but they made me realize how important money issues were in a relationship. I thought about what I was about to do—move in with my boyfriend, the man I suspected I'd marry, sharing expenses and a household. Even though times had changed between 1941 when May married and 1985, how would Adam and I manage all of this?

We move off the chairs onto the sand and start digging a hole, waiting for the water to seep into it, so we can build a sand castle.

~

"May, I really want to try to call Adam on Thursday. He's going to know where we're going. Can we find a payphone?" There was no phone in the condo where we were staying.

"Oh, Shug! Of course!"

Taking both of my hands in hers, she squeezes.

"I'll ask Helen across the way if we can come use her phone. I'm sure she'll let us. You know, her husband was Navy. She knows what it's like."

She reaches over for a hug. Then she clenches her hands into fists and shakes them slightly, a sign of excitement and anticipation. Now I'm not sure who's more eager to make the phone call, her or me.

"I wonder where you'll go?" she muses.

33

A RECIPE FOR GROOM'S CAKE

A year out of college, living in New Orleans, and in our first professional jobs, Adam and I are planning our Aspen wedding. We are definitely on a budget, but that's okay. Our families have generously offered to contribute, but neither of us has the desire to spend gobs of our money—or that of our parents—on a wedding.

To stay within a reasonable budget, we ask May if she will arrange the flowers for the church. Besides being able to sew, home decorate, draw and paint, she is a whiz at arranging flowers, something I cannot seem to do. Her arrangements end up balanced in shape and color while mixing in the perfect amount of greenery. Mine end up looking not-quite-right—just a lump of flowers stuffed into a container. Even though I know something is off, I can never figure out how to fix it. So she is clearly the woman for the job. And she is thrilled to be able to contribute in this way.

She has another idea we love—to have a Groom's Cake—which she herself will make. The groom's cake tradition took off in 19th century Victorian England and became popular in the American South at the same time. Traditionally, these cakes contain fruit or chocolate, and some sort of alcohol. Often it is some version of fruitcake. I know, that sounds gross but hold on a minute. Fruitcake *can* be gross, but it can also be delicious.

May offers to make ours for us from a family recipe from Billy's mother, Granny, the one who spent so many years in the nursing home I hated. Granny was known to be grumpy and not that fun to be around, even before her strokes. But she could *cook*.

During the years before her illness, Thanksgiving was always at Granny's house. The table threatened to give way from the weight of the food piled on it. And a whole separate table threatened the same just from pies, cakes and other desserts. One of those desserts would have been her Nut Cake, which May made for our wedding.

The groom's cake was delicious–sweet with raisins, cherries and dates, crunchy with nuts, spicy with cinnamon and nutmeg, and finished with the subtle tang of bourbon.

Nut Cake (Mrs. Donnelly's/Granny's) Recipe
6 eggs
4 c. plain flour
2 c. sugar
2 sticks butter
1 qt. pecans
1 box raisins
1 box dates
1 small bottle cherries
1 T. baking soda
1 t. nutmeg
1 t. allspice
1 t. salt
1 T. cinnamon
2 c. bourbon, divided

Cream butter and sugar well--add eggs and beat until fluffy.

In big bowl, combine flour, soda and spices. Add this to butter/sugar a small amount at a time.

Add bourbon, raisins, dates, the bottle of cherries with juice, and nuts.

Bake at 275-300 degrees for about 1 1/2 hour. Insert knife to center of cake. Bake until it comes out clean. (Keep a pan of water in the over while baking.)

Saturate the cake with another cup of bourbon after baking. Wrap and seal tightly and store in air tight container. Freezes well.

34

HAVE YOU SEEN CHLOE?

Sometimes I'd say to my mom, "I don't want to go to school today."

I was a good student and liked school—but there were days my introverted side felt overwhelmed by the world, and I'd need a mental health day.

She always said yes.

Sometimes she'd propose the day off. It would usually be a day out. Sometimes to North Park Mall in Dallas, near where we lived. We'd roam the luxuries of Neiman Marcus and then have a ladies lunch at their cafe. But the other thing we'd do is go to the county courthouse and sit in on trials.

We'd duck in, sit down on hard wooden pew-like benches. I was impressed by the cold marble floor, the high ceilings, the judge sitting behind a tall desk in a black robe in front of the room, the solemn hush, the tap, tap, tap of the court reporter recording every word. How did she type so fast?

If it was interesting, we stayed. If not, we wandered to another courtroom, hopefully one that held more drama. Honestly, I always wished we'd chance onto one with more intrigue and mystery than the ones we heard.

I'm not sure I told many friends what we did on those days off. Not the courtroom part at least. I knew enough not to announce this dorky pastime too loudly or widely. I knew it wasn't cool. But it fascinated me.

When I asked my mom recently how she thought of the idea, she said I had been expressing an interest in law, and curiosity about the work of lawyers. "I guess I could have taken you to talk to a lawyer, but since trial law is part of it, I thought it would be interesting," she told me.

It was.

Those days for me were both balm and excitement. Having my mom to myself for a day was the most delicious thing ever. These days were our own, special. They felt secret, a time we walked away from the rules of school and what we "should" be doing and indulged in being together, window shopping, having lunch out. A little vacation in the middle of the week. A little indulgence.

I recall she had trouble getting this sort of "education" to fly with the school. They wouldn't accept this as a legitimate day off, so she just said I was sick.

She reminded me of what Bud would do. He'd come to their house in the morning, offer to take the kids to school, then drive off with no intention of taking them there. He'd make the rounds, picking up cousins and sometimes a few of their friends, until he had a collection of kids on the backseat. Then they would spend the day driving the backroads with him, stopping at multiple filling stations and country stores where Bud seemed to know everyone. Often they'd go to Macon and back, a sixty-mile round trip drive that would take all day with all the stopping, talking, Coca-Cola drinking, and peanut eating.

He'd drive along, window down, wiry tattooed arm perched on the door, cigar in his fingers. When they approached a house or trailer or someone out working in their yard or field, he'd slow the car to a slow roll and shout, "Have ya seen Chloe?"

"Excuse me?"

"Have ya seen *Chloe*?," he'd yell again.

"No!"

"Okay then. Thank you, sir!"

They'd drive off laughing, like they'd just pulled one over on someone.

Why Chloe? I have no idea and neither does my mom. How he thought this one up is anyone's guess. This was vintage Bud. This was all punctuated by more stops at filling stations for visiting and replenishing snacks.

Then on down the road they'd go, asking anybody they could find if they'd seen Chloe. No one had. It was their own joke, their own secret.

One day, they got to Macon and Bud turned onto a wide downtown street. People in other cars started honking, waving and yelling out the window.

"What devil is the matter with them?!" Bud complained.

"You're going the wrong way," people shouted. "Turn around! You can't go this way!"

Unperturbed, Bud shouted back, "Go to hell! I've been coming to Macon all my life and driving this way on this road. I'll be damned if I'm gonna stop now!"

He did what he did, his way. I want to be more like him.

35

HOME SCHOOL

Often when I tell people I homeschooled my kids for eight years, their eyes get big and they say something to the effect of, "Why on *earth* did you do that?!"

So, yes, why? Why would anyone do that?

The truth is that, long before we had kids, the idea of homeschooling intrigued me. My curiosity was piqued by a family who lived outside our little town of Ridgefield, WA who homeschooled their three kids. I'd see them walking together in the nearby wildlife refuge on misty mornings when I was there walking our dogs. Seeing the kids with their mom tugged at something in me.

Sitting next to May and her sister Betty on long car trips, I had learned to embroider and sew. In college, I learned to knit from friends as we sat bundled up against the Vermont cold, sipping tea in someone's dorm room. From my dad I learned to use tools, how to measure, how to swim and play various sports, how to make stained glass. With my stepmom, I learned to measure flour, grease cookie sheets, and turn out melty chocolate chip cookies. With my mom and stepdad, there were evenings of long conversations at the dinner table where I learned everything from the entirety of the digestive system to how fun it was to play word games, to how to have a productive debate (even if a lot of times I ended up in tears because I couldn't hold my own). And of course there were those mental health days that Mom and I spent at the courthouse.

However, it wasn't until my oldest was in an "academic" kindergarten that didn't allow running on the blacktop of the playground (no *running*??!!) that my husband and I decided to make the leap to homeschooling. The light had gone out in Levi's eyes.

After I told Levi's teacher about our decision, I walked out of the school with his little hand in mine. My body felt lighter. I could breathe again. We got soup and sandwiches at Panera Bread and sat in a booth where we played a game called Frog Juice. Together we deciphered the instructions, figured out the rules, and played several rounds.

Once we started homeschooling, my two kids and I spent our days walking to the park, riding bikes, hiking, going on field trips to the science center, the art and train museum, spending time with other homeschoolers at parks and playgrounds. We watched MythBusters and played lots of games. We grocery shopped and weighed vegetables and read nutrition labels. We measured ingredients and stirred and cooked. The kids did basic math as they spent their money at Target.

It often reminded me of my own childhood, of a freedom lost to many of today's children. When I was a kid, I had designated "creek shoes" for wading in the stream that ran through the greenway in my neighborhood, where we tromped around pretending to be Lewis and Clark. My friends and I found an old tree house we took over as our own. In this pre-cell-phone time, no one knew where we were except "at the creek" or "riding our bikes." Those territories extended for miles. We knew to be home by dinner time.

Monopoly games went on for days between me, my friend, Lori, and her brothers and sisters. We pogo-sticked and roller skated up and down the block. We built houses out of refrigerator boxes Lori's dad brought home for us. We built traps and tried to catch birds. We found dead birds and mice and held funerals. We held weddings. I married Kevin Lemmons more than once.

We played. And played and played and played.

I wanted that kind of life for my own kids. I wanted to see Levi's black eyes sparkle again. And I wanted that kind of life for me too. It had taken a very long time to form this family with infertility challenges and then the adoption of our children. I wanted more time with them—yearned for just a few more stolen moments.

Maybe that's how Mom felt when she took me to the courthouse. Or when Bud hauled a car full of kids to Macon and back.

36

MEANEST MOM ON EARTH

When Levi, our first-born, was a few months old, we were still playing the let-him-fall-asleep-in-our-arms-and-then-try-to-put-him-into-the-crib-without-waking-him game, and it wasn't working. I would sit in the rocker, read or sing to Levi, then give him his last bottle. He'd doze off, his slight weight sinking into me as all his muscles relaxed. I could feel his release as he sank deeper and deeper. Holding his warm weight against me made my own eyes flutter and dip. At some point, I had to put him down, although a part of me wanted to sit there staring at him and holding him forever.

The path to holding him in my arms had been a long one. Years not conceiving, doctor's visits, medications, and multiple surgeries to remove ovarian cysts. Then, in what turned out to be an adoption process of eight months, shorter than human gestation, here he was.

Like all parents, we considered him to be beautiful and perfect.

What wasn't so perfect was this process of putting him down for the night. I'd wait until I thought he was deeply asleep, then creep to the crib, put him down s-l-o-w-l-y. Then wait. Then gently extract an arm while my other hand pressed gently on his belly. Then, ever so lightly, I'd release the weight of my hand on his stomach. At first, this worked. But soon, when his back touched the bed, his eyes would fly open and, highly offended, he'd shriek. And I'd start the process over.

It was clear we needed to have the nerve to put him down and let him learn to settle himself to sleep. But it was so painful and hard. The few times we tried it, Adam or I would freak out and pick him up. When I heard him cry, my chest hurt. A physical force inside my body propelled me to scoop him out of the crib. Bedtime was getting more and more protracted and more and more frustrating. It was clear we couldn't keep on like this. And yet, as a team, we couldn't seem to get it together to stay the course.

I read and reread books on sleep training, how to kindly help your baby learn to calm himself by letting him cry for a certain amount of time, return to comfort but not pick him up, and then leave him again. The books and friends who had been through it assured me it would work. Something had to work, because we were spending an hour helping him go to sleep at night. It interrupted our dinner and evening time together. And it wasn't helping him learn how to take care of himself.

"Mom, this is awful. I know what we need to do, but we just can't seem to do it. Adam's going out of town soon and I'm going to try it again while he's gone. But I'm still afraid I won't be able to stand his cries. It breaks my heart and makes me feel like the meanest mom on earth."

"I tell you what," she said to me. "I'm going to be in Milledgeville with May while Adam is gone. You call us one night when you put him down and we'll help you through it."

"Deal."

~

On the appointed evening, I got myself prepared. On the kitchen counter was my vodka and o.j. in a cut crystal glass (it would be cocktail hour for them and I figured I needed a little something to bolster my nerve), the small, portable white plastic baby monitor, the handset for the cordless phone, and my kitchen timer.

I went through the bedtime routine with Levi, put him into the crib and raced out of the room as he began to cry. I rounded the corner to the kitchen, plinked some ice into my glass, grabbed everything and went out into the summer evening light and hopped into the passenger side of our red VW van. I had to be somewhere I couldn't hear the crying. I wondered what the neighbors would think if they saw me sitting in the car, talking on the phone and drinking while clutching a baby monitor.

I dialed May's phone number, the same one I'd been calling for my entire thirty-eight years. I imagined them in May's living room, their own cocktails in hand. Just thinking of the two of them together in that familiar space helped my heartbeat calm a little.

Mom answered the phone. "Hello?"

"Meanest mom on earth here."

"Where are you?" she asked.

"In the car in the driveway. With my drink and the baby monitor. Turned off."

"Okay, you can do this. And you aren't mean. You're doing a good thing for Levi, yourself, and Adam."

"Ugh! I wish it felt that way. This is so hard."

"Hey, Shug!" May said after picking up the other receiver. "You're the best little mama. Don't you worry about this."

We chatted back and forth while I watched the timer count down ten minutes that felt like ten hours.

"Okay, moment of truth."

I reached for the monitor sitting on the dashboard, turned it on and . . .

We all listened.

Silence.

"Woo hoo!"

"Yippee! You did it! I knew you could do this," they both told me. "You're so strong!"

"Thanks, you two. I couldn't have done it without you. Any of it. I love you."

"We love you too! Stay sweet."

37

WILL YOU ACCEPT A COLLECT CALL?

By the time I'm nine or ten, I'm free to use the phone on my own.

I dial "O" for Operator.

"I'd like to make a collect call to xxx-xxx-xxxx," I say.

"Certainly. Who's calling please?"

"Chris Chandler."

After a few rings, May's voice comes onto the line with a hello.

"Will you accept a collect call from Chris Chandler?"

"Of course."

"Hey, Shug!," she says to me. "So good to hear your voice."

We'll repeat this thousands of times over the years until I'm old enough to fund my own phone bills.

I call her with the good, the bad, and the mundane. I tell her about new record albums I've bought, about how Ruth and I sit on each other's bedroom floors pouring over album notes. I share tidbits I've gleaned about who sings back up or who plays the drums. I tell her about sleepovers, who's nice and who's mean and whose bra got soaked in water and frozen. How Ruth and I have a half-way spot where we walk to meet up with one another: the big oak tree in front of Laurie's house. I tell her about the boy I have a crush on in sixth grade. And then the boy I start going "steady" with, and how he gives me a St. Christopher medal. How he holds my hand in class in the dark when a history movie is playing, but later I find out he's done it on a dare and I break up with him via emissary, sending Ruth to return his necklace. Over the phone, I cry to May over the insult of it. I celebrate with her when I learn to do a back walk-over on the beam in gymnastics. I complain to her and garner support when my parents say "no" to staying out late, to sleepovers two nights in a row, to making me wait to get my ears pierced. We share the day-to-day. Most of it is not big or profound. What matters is our ongoing connection and presence for one another.

About whoever has been unfair or mean or unpleasant (to my way of seeing it), May always says, "Oh, Shug. You know I love you. You just tell them to stick it in their ear! Stay sweet!"

38

MEMORY HILL CEMETERY

"What would you like to do today, Sugar?" May and Billy often asked when I visited them. My answer: "Let's go to the cemetery!"

In my family, this was and is a normal request. I still love to visit the old cemetery in Milledgeville and never think of it as an odd thing to do until I return from my vacation and begin to recount the adventures of the visit to my birth home. As I tell about the cemetery, I see the person I am speaking to gazing at me with eyes wide, eyebrows raised in expectation, waiting for me to get to the exciting part. They don't understand—this *is* the exciting part.

The old Memory Hill Cemetery lies on a mostly flat, 20-acre piece of land near the center of Milledgeville. Once a public square, it was designated a cemetery in 1803. The streets of this little town are lined with antebellum homes of white clapboard with tall, fluted columns. They have wrap-around porches set with rocking chairs and fan windows above the front doors. They still bear the names of the generational families who lived there—Hinson, Sanford, Bell. People tell of the ghosts who still inhabit them, like the woman who roams her garden at dusk or twilight, looking for the silver she buried there to hide it from the Union soldiers.

The cemetery is mostly full of old graves, although there are new ones too. A wrought-iron fence borders it. There is a large arched gate at the entrance. Some plots within the cemetery are also surrounded by smaller iron fences, some people inside their fences alone, but mostly with other members of their family. Bricks, made locally from the red Georgia clay, make retaining walls for some of the areas that are built up a foot or so above the others.

"Which one do you want to see first?' May and Billy ask me. "The Train Robber!"

So it always was and always will be—one of my favorite dead people, a train robber, who lived and died in the days when train robber was an occupation. I wished so badly that I could talk to him, hear about his adventures. I would have asked him how he did it—did he ride alongside on a horse and ambush the train, or go aboard as a passenger and then hold them up? Why did he do it? I imagined him to be Butch Cassidy-like, a "good" robber, not to be feared, but to be admired. In my mind he wore a 10-gallon hat, had dark graying hair, a bushy mustache, a swagger in his cowboy-booted walk, and a red bandana around his neck.

I learned many years later, from a small book on Milledgeville's history, that his name was Bill Miner and he was known as "The Grey Fox." He was born in 1843 in Kansas and died in the State Penitentiary in Milledgeville in 1914, which is how he came to be buried at Memory Hill. I guess train robbing didn't pay in the long run.

On the way to and from the Train Robber, we pass another friend, an unmarked vault built from red brick with an arched concrete roof and a wooden door. The mortar is falling from between the bricks, leaving dark holes into which I peer, desperately hoping, and desperately afraid, to see bones. Billy and I always walk up to this one and say, "Helloooo," hoping our long-dead friend will respond in kind.

My other friend is a man whose large tombstone tells the story of his death—killed at Andrew Jackson's funeral, run over by a cannon that backfired during the 21-cannon salute.

Some markers are grand, above-ground vaults built of marble with angels or women in flowing robes on top. Others are flat stones of marble—gray, white, pink. Some soldiers who lie there are remembered by a small white marble marker with a bronze emblem attached, sometimes with a small flag flying there. Others, many old, look as though they were made by pouring fine concrete into a mold and then engraved.

Memory Hill contains over 8900 graves, over 7700 identifiable. The amount of history here is stunning—statesmen and leaders, the author and Milledgeville resident Flannery O'Connor, patients from Milledgeville's Central State Hospital, and even Milledgeville resident Charles Bonner's favorite dogs, Nick and Bruno, buried there in 1926 and 1931. But most importantly to me, it is also the final resting place of my Grandfather and Grandmother Chandler. May and Billy lie in a different cemetery in Milledgeville.

Cemeteries can seem like sad and scary places—unless you have friends there.

39

THE ONE ABOUT THE SOFA

One time when my mom was a teenager, she went into Wea Wea and Bud's living room. "Wea Wea! Where's the living room furniture?"

"Sugar," Wea Wea said, "I've been wondering the same thing myself! I don't know what happened to it!"

"Did you give it to somebody?"

"No darlin', I don't think so."

Turns out Wea Wea and Bud had sent the sofa out for reupholstering but the man had taken *all* the living room furniture--and failed to return it.

40

THE LANGUAGE OF FAMILY

My first weeks at college were filled with crushing homesickness. I made some tearful phone calls home. Mom held steady and reminded me of something she'd been talking me through for years: that night time is the hardest time. That it will all seem better by the light of day. And, of course, she was right.

I settled in. Slowly I built a family there.

Because I lived far away, friends took me in for Thanksgiving, Spring Break, and long weekends. I was lucky enough over the years to be lugged home to Boston, Maine, Washington, DC, Charleston, and Westchester County, NY. I watched other mothers and fathers navigate getting dinner on the table and the kitchen cleaned up. I saw extended families negotiate Thanksgiving, felt the tense moments, saw who drank too much, who pulled a notecard out of their pocket and made notes during a meal (still don't know what that was about.) I watched siblings reunite and spar. I developed a crush on a girlfriend's brother and tried not to stare too hard or be too jealous when he'd return in the evening with his high school sweetheart. I sat at tables where silences were long and uncomfortable, the loudest sound forks scraping the plates.

I went home with a friend for Thanksgiving during my second year at school. We were all expected to dress up to a degree I found uncomfortably formal. The conversation was stiff and stilted. My fancy linen shirt itched. One of the parents and one of the siblings drank too much at every meal. There were lots of things moving around between family members, lots of expressions and eye rolls, silences and sighs. Communications I could only guess the meaning of.

I was learning that each family had its own language.

41

I'M HAPPY RIGHT HERE

My friend Carol and her two sisters went to camp for nine weeks every summer. Why they would want to leave home for that long was a mystery to me. I heard all the stories of canoeing and campfires, learned the songs, saw the crafts they made. They loved it and waited eagerly to go each summer.

I'd sit with Carol after school let out for summer, the big trunk in her room slowly getting filled with all the things she'd need for her time away. I'd watch an identical one fill up in her big sister's room. Plus an eager little sister waiting until she'd be old enough to go off with them too. But none of it pulled at me.

I was one of those kids who took a long time to successfully sleep over at someone's house. Don't get me wrong: the idea sounded fun, and I wanted to go. I'd pack my pajamas and head off happily and without nervousness. But then it would start to get dark. Bedtime would come. A shakiness would start inside my stomach and chest and head, a feeling like the world was sliding sideways. I felt unanchored, alone. And then the worst —I would start to cry. I tried so hard to deny the feeling, to stop the tears from rising. but I couldn't. Sometimes it was before bedtime. But often we had been tucked in, lights out, parents in their own room behind a closed door. Not only did I feel miserable and like the world was about to end, but then I had to embarrass myself by telling my friend, who would then traipse with me to her mom and dad.

I'd insist I wanted to go home.

Sometimes this feeling would come over me even when I was just playing at a friend's house, all going well, everyone happy and getting along. Out of nowhere, an internal voice would say: *I want to go home. NOW.*

Sometimes still, as an adult at sixty years old, I'll be out doing errands or hanging out with friends. I'm fine. And then I'm not. It's the same overwhelming feeling that seems to fly up out of nowhere. It doesn't creep up slowly. It doesn't give me warning. It swoops in and insists it's time to go.

Home—the physical place and the people in it—is my safe space and still the place I still most want to be. Just the other night, in bed under the covers, book in my hand and a dog leaning heavily against my leg, I said to my husband, "*This is all I need. I could stay right here forever and be happy.*"

42

THE ONE ABOUT THE SHOES

Wea Wea was sitting in the rocking chair in May's living room with her legs crossed. I looked down at her feet and was confused. Something didn't look right. Although her legs were crossed, her feet looked as if they weren't.

"Wea Wea, you have your shoes on the wrong feet," I said to her.

"That's okay, Sugar. They're more comfortable that way."

She had also cut holes into the sides of the shoes to make room for her bunions. She never complained and she wasn't going to complain that her shoes hurt her feet either. She just took care of it and kept on.

43

HIDE & PEEP

May and Billy's house was a small, one-story home of red brick. The carport was on the right. The main part of the house ran to the left with a long narrow porch running all the way along the front. On the left side, a small section jutted out toward the front, holding two bedrooms and May's bathroom. There were high shuttered windows above the porch. May's bathroom window looked out toward the front of the house and the porch.

Elsie, who lived next door, seemed to lie in wait for anyone to leave the house. May studiously avoided her. Not easy, since Elsie would often be outside raking or pulling weeds, ready to dash over and talk. And once she got started, it wasn't easy to stop her. She didn't take a hint well, going on and on as we squirmed and politely tried to take our leave. From her bathroom window, May could see the front porch and Elsie's yard so it was the perfect place for surveillance before leaving the house or to see who was knocking at the door.

If there was a knock on the door, May would run back to her bathroom to "peep," as she called it, out the window. Or sometimes she would peek out of one of the high windows in the living room. If it was someone else she wanted to avoid (and that seemed like just about anyone who knocked), we would sneak into the back part of the house until the person went away.

May was quite social. But only when and with whom she wanted to be. For my entire life, I was schooled in this method of avoidance of unwanted neighbors and knockers. It was totally normal for May to stage-whisper, "It's Elsie!" Or for her to hear a knock on the door and utter, "Oh, *shoot!*" like it was the worst thing in the world for someone to knock on the door. We would quietly scurry away from windows and doors until they were gone.

Most of my family falls into the category of what my mom has termed "gregarious hermits." We like being around people outside the family—to a point. But once that point is reached, we retreat to recharge.

After Billy's funeral, there were still lots of family gathered in the living room, including my mom and stepdad. It was late afternoon and all non-family callers had left. We were still in our dress-up clothes, but in our stocking feet, shoes kicked off, winding down in the living room with snacks and glasses of wine.

Knock, knock, knock. May peeped out of the high window in front.

"It's Elsie!"

Everyone in the family got up and quietly ran into the den or the back of the house without saying a word. Only my stepfather was left sitting in the living room wondering what had just happened. Clearly, we had failed to fill him in on this family habit.

44

VANCOUVER BARRACKS

The huge expanse of lusciously green lawn at the Vancouver Barracks in Vancouver, Washington is sprinkled with tall, far reaching Douglas fir that spread their friendly arms wide and create shade. They are the most elegant of trees, reminding me of tall ladies in flowing robes. There are also some deciduous trees, mostly along the edges of the lawn. Largely though, there is wide-open, sun-covered, spring-green, uninterrupted grass running down a gentle slope. It is not enough to drive up to it. I must get out and sit on it, take off my shoes and feel its cool, moist softness on my bare feet.

There is a small playground with swings and a jungle gym. Nearby sits a shelter with picnic tables. Almost daily there is a group of kids in a summer day camp who spend their lunchtime here. Today they're scattered in small groups under the trees eating orange, green, and red popsicles. Their teachers yell to them to sit down with their popsicles, but they cannot resist what is my own temptation: to run across the grass with arms spread wide, face to the sun, hair flying, and roll down the hill until gravity can pull them no farther. The open space invites abandon, whispers in your ear telling you to run wild, turn cartwheels, lose control. Maybe that's why I like to write here.

I have another kinship with this place. The name of this place wove in and out of my childhood, showed up in black-and-white photos pulled from the bottom drawer of a dresser full of pictures from across the years, turned up in stories told by May and Billy about Billy's early days in the Army when they were stationed here prior to his going overseas during WWII. All my life, I heard about Vancouver Barracks, saw pictures of the white clapboard officer's quarters surrounded by wraparound porches. I heard how May, as a young newlywed, along with a friend, bought a freshly killed chicken to fry for a picnic at the Oregon coast with their husbands. How they plucked and cleaned the chicken, fried it up, and packed it for eating. How there was something they hadn't known about properly cleaning and plucking a chicken and how, when they took their first bites, they found stiff feather ends still in the skin.

But to me, it remained placeless, contextless, a place from long ago, a mystery, simply a name. In 1990, my husband and I moved to Vancouver, in southwest Washington State. It sits just across the Columbia River from Portland, OR and is the location of Ft. Vancouver and the Barracks. We had been living in Alexandria, VA, me working my first professional job in mental health, he in the Coast Guard and working at CG Headquarters in Washington, DC. He was awaiting orders to the Marine Safety office in Seattle, a move we were excited about, eager to be closer to the mountains and oceans of the Pacific Northwest. But a diagnosis of Type I diabetes for him put an end to his Coast Guard career. Still, we made our way to the Northwest, albeit a bit farther south than originally planned.

So this is how I find myself living in the town where the

Barracks are located, this once-mysterious and placeless location now a part of my daily life. I frequently drive by here as I go about my work day, eat my lunch on the lawn in the summer, and find myself drawn to just being here. It took me a while to make the connection, that *this* Vancouver, *this* Ft. Vancouver, *this* Vancouver Barracks were the same as *that* one, that one I heard about, fingered photos of, tried to imagine and place on the literal and figurative map.

May visited me once when I lived here. We walked through the Barracks and stood in front of the Salvation Army boarding house just a block off the Barracks property where she and Billy had rented a room, a large two-story home painted a light yellow. And sometime later, my mom and I were able to go inside, to walk up the creaking wooden staircase to what had been May and Billy's second story room with windows looking out the front of the house onto the street, to see the painted wooden floor, to see how for so many years, residents had continued to paint around the bed, leaving an unpainted brown rectangle on the floor. To stand in the room where my mom was conceived.

I marvel at the way life has circled around in this way, bringing me here to a place so far from Georgia, to one of the few other places May and Billy lived in their entire lives. What are the chances? I want to say it's a coincidence I ended up here, and then I wonder, is it random? Or are there forces out there serving reconnection, forces that circle us back around to our histories in ways we aren't aware of, that we don't control?

The Officers' Quarters are beautifully restored and the whole property is inviting with its open lawns, the vista to the south over old Ft. Vancouver (originally established by the Hudson's Bay Company during the settlement of the American West) and down the gently sloping hill to the Columbia River.

It feels like some sort of miracle to connect these mysterious dots and to spend my days with my feet walking the same sidewalks my grandparents walked fifty years before. I love the sense of connection, feeling like I could pull them in around me at any time just by sitting here staring out at the view or driving through the Barracks or by the old boarding house. Like something in the air still holds parts of them, like I can breathe it in, wrap it about me just by visiting.

I look at the elegant houses on Officers Row, neatly restored, their wooden siding painted a light tan, their wide porches wrapping around them with off-white trim and banisters, wide wooden steps leading down to the lawn. If I hold very still, I can see, in my mind's eye, my handsome young grandfather standing on the porch in his khaki uniform, his dark, wavy hair neatly combed back, his black eyes shining. Billy holds his cap under one arm. His other circles May's waist. Her dress is the faintest blue, matching her eyes. They step off the porch. He places his cap on his head. He offers his arm and she takes it as they walk down the steps, onto the sidewalk, and slowly fade away.

45

A RECIPE FOR HOE CAKE

Grandmother Chandler made hoe cake, a thin unleavened cake made of cornmeal, water and salt and originally baked on the flat surface of a "griddle hoe" over an open fire. Contrary to common myth, it's not called hoe cake because it was cooked on the blade of a hoe in the fields, though maybe that happened in a pinch.

Grandmother made hers in a cast iron skillet. She would mix the batter and then pour it into the dark black skillet, sizzling with a thin layer of oil. It would spread into a thin layer over the bottom of the skillet, all the way to the edges. The middle would remain thicker than the edges, maybe 1/4 inch, and tender. But my oh-so-favorite part was the edge. Being thinner, it fried in the oil into a crispy-crunchy lace. Covered in butter while still hot, it was heaven. I would have fought someone for the edge. Being the only grandchild for many years, I was probably granted more than my fair share of this delicacy.

Hoecake by Sarah Chandler

- *white cornmeal*
- *water*
- *salt*

1. Add enough water to the cornmeal and salt to make the mixture "gooshy" (her word).
2. Heat oil in skillet and pour in batter. Fry until middle is cooked and edges are crispy.

Sadly, I have not successfully recreated this dish in my own kitchen, partly because I have yet to figure out exactly what consistency "gooshy" is, and partly because I am still trying to figure out how hot to heat the skillet and how much batter to pour in.

This is one of those dishes you need to learn by doing, and I sincerely regret not learning this one from her.

46

SECRET PROCESS

In December 2019, we took a family trip to Mt. Rushmore. I bought South Dakota raw clover honey at the gift store. The next morning in our cabin, I saw soft butter sitting on the counter next to my new jar of honey.

A memory came back to me.

Grandaddy Chandler used to spread what he called Secret Process on my biscuits or toast in the morning. He said the fairies came to make it and no one could watch them or they wouldn't come. I had to sit under the dining room table while they made it. In fact, Secret Process was soft butter mixed with honey. I'm not sure at what point I figured that out but I would never have admitted I knew the secret. If Grandaddy were alive today, I'd still be willing to climb under the dining room table just to keep the magic alive.

I stood in that cabin in South Dakota spreading Secret Process on my toast, biting into dripping butter and honey, and I was back in that kitchen in Georgia. I just wished it was a big fat biscuit I was biting into.

My sixteen year-old son was still asleep on the pull-out couch on the sofa bed. I wondered why I had never made him sit under the table while the fairies came, the same way I did as a child, as my dad did as a little boy. I asked my dad recently if this was something Grandaddy made up or if someone had done it for him. His answer: "This was totally Dad's."

~

Granddaddy was a curiosity to me. A teaser and joker—not in a mean sense—but there was often humor going on and even though I knew that, I often didn't understand the joke.

He said things I absolutely did not understand—and yet I did. As an exclamation, he'd slap his leg and say, "Well, cat snagged my purple blue jeans!" I never knew what in the *hell* that meant except I got the gist. It was surprise; his "wow."

There was a swing set in their backyard. I'd beg and beg to be pushed on the swing. "Granddaddy push me! Granddaddy push me!" He'd say to me, "Is my name Granddaddy Push Me?!" But he always came outside with me.

When it was time for me to let the swing stop and come inside, he'd say, "Okay now. Let the cat die down." (I know— there seems to be a thing with cats, right?) I knew he was saying it was time to let the swing glide to a stop, but why he said it that way, I never knew. And though I always wondered about it, I never asked. I just knew what he meant.

~

Grandaddy was obsessed with a few things—typewriters, propane gas, Polaroid cameras, and fishing.

He owned a business that sold propane and he was BIG on gas stoves, grills and anything else that ran on propane.

He always had a Polaroid camera. It was thrilling to me every time he took it out.

As with my experience of the rest of him, there seemed to

be a fair amount of mystery in the development process of the Polaroids. I have vague memories of the partially developed photos being shut between two sheets of aluminum and, if it was cold out, the necessity of warming the developing negative under an armpit.

In the early days of these cameras, the film came out of the camera and then a certain amount of waiting time—30 or 60 seconds—I can't remember—before Grandaddy pulled the paper back from the surface to reveal the still-developing photo underneath. He would hold it by the tab, careful not to touch the part that contained the actual photo. He timed the wait for the development on his wristwatch, a silver and gold watch with a stretchy metal band that flopped slightly on his wiry wrist as he turned his arm over to see the gold second hand tick around.

Then the moment of truth. Slowly he'd pull, separating the photo from the black sheet that came off, sticky with emulsion, the chemicals that helped the photo develop.

He'd stand, the sticky paper in one hand, the photo in the other, waving the paper gently through the air to encourage drying, holding it by the corner, careful not to get his fingers on the photo while it dried.

It was like a magic trick. Pulling and clicking, waiting and timing, the flourish with which he seemed to pull the film from the camera, the clicking sound as the film emerged, the fantastic anticipation of it all. One was always as miraculous as the next, a photo slowly materializing as we stood and stared, the colors getting brighter, the image clearer.

I see us standing in the backyard under the tall pines. I feel the velvet weight of moist air. I smell the scent of pine. I am a little girl, awed and mystified by this man who has tamed a squirrel to eat peanuts out of his hand, who uses expressions I kind of understand but kind of don't, and who makes photos appear.

Grandaddy also loved to fish. He had some land outside of town where he had a small pond he stocked with fish. He'd go out there to fish and sometimes took me with him. I loved just being with him, but that also meant fishing. I didn't get it, the satisfaction of it. Perhaps because I was squeamish about baiting my hook with those live, squirmy, slimy worms. And perhaps because I rarely caught anything. He used to tell me I didn't catch any fish because I wasn't holding my mouth right. I never did figure out how to hold my mouth, which is probably why I still don't get fishing.

There were three bedrooms in Grandmother and Grandaddy's house. Their bedroom, the "back" bedroom which had been my Aunt Sally's, and the middle room, right off the den, which had been my dad's. There wasn't much evidence left of my dad's inhabitation of the space but there were fascinating pieces of evidence of Grandaddy. I loved to rifle through the closet in that room to find the treasures left behind.

There was an electric typewriter there—of course. Also in that closet, and pawed over by me each and every time I slept there, was a small set of the most highly exotic things in the world: a set of bongo drums; a collection of arrowheads found by Grandaddy and my dad; and the rattle from a snake. These items spoke to me of other worlds—of Africans beating drums somewhere far away, dancing in a circle, bodies painted and earlobes heavy with beads like I had seen in the pages of National Geographic; of Native Americans roaming the land and hunting, exciting me with the idea that maybe I had placed my feet in the same places they had placed theirs; and the thrilling danger of a poisonous snake my grandfather had actually caught and killed.

Mystery and magic.

47

WHEN IT'S MAGIC

A fuzzy memory sits in my mind. I'm about three years old, at home, on a bench at the picnic table that served as our dining room table. I sit next to my mom, paper in front of me and pencil in hand, scratching lines of letters onto the paper.

"What does that spell? Does that spell something? What does that spell?" I ask over and over.

I already understand that these marks on the page add up to things called words. That strings of words make sentences. That strings of sentences make stories.

At some point I finally figure out the code and join the club of readers. Letters and words and reading and writing become a fundamental part of my days.

It doesn't take long for letter writing to become part of my life. When I am four years old, we move to Texas. All my grandparents remain in Georgia. Long-distance calling is expensive, paid for by the call and the cost varies depending on the hour of the day you are calling. We often write letters instead.

At age fifteen, I write to May in neat cursive on a piece of lined notebook paper:

> *May,*
>
> *Hi! How are you? I am very happy! We are taking exams this week. Today we took history & science . . . Tomorrow I'll take my math & english exams. They should be easy too!*
>
> *I also got my phone today! Finally! My number is 234-0808. That's pretty easy to remember.*

I go on to tell her about buying Stevie Wonder's new album, *Songs in the Key of Life,* and I write out the entire lyrics of one of his songs from that record, "When It's Magic."

I wax poetic about how great the song is—how great *all* his songs are —and how much he's able to say in the several minutes that make up a song. (I still agree with my fifteen-year-old self on this.)

And, I end, of course, with "I love you." I hear her response to me in my head, her usual, "Stay sweet."

These days, I frequently drive past the bank of mailboxes at the entrance to my neighborhood without stopping. They practically shout at me, "Nothing to see here!" My box is most likely filled with junk mail, bills, a magazine I never read from my rural utility district, ditto a mailing from AAA and AARP, requests from various alma maters for donations, postcards from local real estate agents reminding us of their existence, and more requests for money from political organizations.

I do enjoy the occasional print catalog from Sundance or Title Nine—cue drooling over jewelry or clothes I rarely buy. Notice I didn't say never. But that's nothing to rush to the mailbox for.

Today, most interesting things come from UPS or the Amazon driver. Almost all compelling correspondence comes via email or text. While I do enjoy things about the speed and downright marvel of my words flying immediately through the ether to the person on the other side, I'm sad my physical mailbox holds so little allure.

All those years ago when my on-paper letter writing was frequent, the metal mailbox sticking up out of the grass by the street was a thing of beauty and excitement. I'd walk out the front door of the house, down the concrete sidewalk cutting the lawn in half, step down the curb into the street to stand in front of the box, pull the tongue-shaped door open and reach inside to see what it held. Later, when we moved to Colorado, our personal mail came to my stepdad's office four blocks from home. I either waited eagerly for him to cart it home or dashed the four blocks, popped into the back door leading directly to the business office, chatted with the receptionist, rifled through the mail, and took it back home. College found me with a mailbox of my own in the cinder block basement of an older dorm, where I'd stand eagerly twisting and turning the little scored knob until the door swung open.

Whatever the receptacle for my mail, going to check it was exciting, because there might be a letter. A handwritten one, most likely on stationery, a card, sometimes simple notebook paper, maybe a postcard. Maybe something from May or Grandmother Chandler, my earliest correspondents, maybe something from a friend.

It's thrilling to pick a hand-addressed envelope out of the mailbox. The outside of the letter holds each person's distinctive scrawl, as unique to them as their fingerprints. It's the first tell as to who it's from. As I hold an envelope in my hand, a tingle rises in my chest, my insides smile and so does my face.

❧

I've recently started writing letters and cards again. Just a few weeks ago, I was rewarded for stopping to collect the mail by a white envelope bearing the return address of Ruth, one of my oldest friends. I smiled. My heart did a little flip and leap. Yay! A response to the letter I had sent her. I was tempted to get into my car, tear it open, and read it right then and there. But I decided to savor the moment. To carry it home, make a cup of tea, sit and slowly open it, to notice the texture and crinkle of unfolding. To once again see handwriting I would recognize anywhere.

The joy of a letter, one on paper, is the tangibility of it; the knowledge this paper was brushed by the sender's skin, the ink put there by the movement of their hand and transported to me; the physical exchange of *this* paper, these words I hold in *my* hands now. I can carry them with me and re-read them as I sit with my own paper and pen to respond. I can put the letter in a shoebox or bind it with a rubber band, put it under my bed and have it there any time to return to. I can touch it, feel the texture of the paper with my fingertips. It's real.

A bundle of letters Adam and I exchanged after we were married but unexpectedly geographically separated for a year sits tied in a ribbon in a memento box in the basement. I have a handful of my own letters May kept, found after she died, in a large manila envelope marked "Save" in her handwriting. When I come across any of these, I delight in the time travel back to former selves, enjoy being dipped back into age fifteen, seventeen, twenty-four. There are some cringe-worthy moments, like the discovery of way too many exclamation points, but mostly the encounters with former-me make me smile and feel a tenderness for the younger one. It also makes me wish more of them had been saved, that I had more of these touchstones with the past.

48

PHOTOGRAPHIC MEMORIES

A small bowl of wooden apples sits on a table in my living room, a collection May built for me over the years. I dust them one by one, gently with a cloth. Turn them over in my hands and set them gently back in the bowl.

I loved her house—eclectic and personal, warm and easy, nice but not formal, and unlike so many other homes I thought were either over-decorated and impersonal or just not thought about. She knew how to combine the old with the new, how to use pattern and color as a splash before a "pop" of color was a thing, and she was not held captive to decorating trends. Her look was her own, using what she had and what she liked to make an inviting space.

One piece of furniture that was in her living room my entire life was a long, low, dark and heavy coffee table with sides that folded down almost to the floor. I could crawl through it from end to end as a child. On it always sat a huge wide wooden bowl with her apple collection—two dozen hand-carved, hand-painted apples made by Sara Finney, a local wood carver known for her carvings of apples and birds. I would wiggle into the space below the table and pretend to be under a car, repairing it. Something about the dark cave of the underside of the table held an appeal that never wore off.

Shuttered windows ran high on the wall along the front of the house, starting at about five feet and going up a foot or so. The back of the living room was spanned by sliding doors, allowing a view across a large pine-tree covered lot to a small lake. At some point, a fireplace with a brick hearth was added at one end of the room. A large table stood behind an armchair with a lamp. The couch had a high back. A variety of armchairs and a couch carried varied prints.

A small desk with a pull-down front perched between a hallway opening and the kitchen doorway, the place Billy sat to pay bills. He did this very methodically, taking out the large green binder that held sheets of checks divided by scored lines. I can see him remove the pen from his shirt pocket, hear the click as he pressed the top to pop the ink cartridge out, see his large, neat script run across the lines as he wrote names and numbers. I can taste the glue on the envelopes and stamps he let me lick. The precision and neatness of the process fascinated me. The little drawer holding the stamps, the slot for envelopes, the way they were piled neatly on top of one another waiting to go to the mailbox. I think I channel him each time I sit down at my own desk to pay bills.

Billy's father was known as Pa Donnelly to his family. His pocket watch hung in a glass bell that sat on the top of the desk. Until someone stole it during a party. May always suspected a relative who was also rumored to steal silver place settings.

An old bureau with hammered brass hardware stood in one corner of the living room. The bottom drawer held decades worth of loose family photos. One of my favorite things was to grab photos by the handful and sit with May & Billy on the floor or couch while they told me who was in the photos and recounted stories about the people, places, and events.

Photos of my mom at four years old on a pallet outside on the lawn when they lived in California and she was recovering from rheumatic fever; the oh-so-handsome young Billy with his black eyes and dark bushy eyebrows in his WWII khaki uniform; May, twenty-something, in a white bathing suit on a Florida beach during the time Billy was overseas; photos of my mom as an infant and young child with my May and Billy, Wea Wea and Bud and Ma and Fa Hawkins, her great-grandparents; photos of me as a baby. Piles and piles of them, no order, just randomly thumbed through. The only order Billy insisted on was that the names of those in the picture, the date, and the location be noted on the back of the photo. I used to bristle at his meticulousness about this, to consider it some annoying adult thing. Now when I come across a photo and wonder who those people are, when or where it was taken, I can often thank Billy that the information I'm craving is on the back, often in his hand. Or in mine, since I learned the habit from him.

I still like the days of print photos better than digital. Digital photos get stored away on someone's computer and sometimes never seen again. You can't rummage through them by the handful. Which is why I also object to photos in albums. I like to paw through them. I love the surprise of what the next handful brings, the thrill of finding old favorites and the anticipation and mystery of what will turn up next. I like to touch them, hold them. It makes memories more tangible.

I pick a red wooden apple from my bowl and turn its cool roundness in my hands.

49

SPRING BREAK

I'm a freshman at Middlebury College. I've never been colder in my life. The dampness is bone-biting in a way the dry Colorado cold rarely is. Also missing the Colorado sunshine. The temps here drop to below-zero lows I've never experienced and stay that way for weeks on end.

Having no car, I walk everywhere—out across the flat windy expanse to one of the dining units, downtown for errands or dinner out, across campus to class, or the pool for exercise.

I've learned the true benefit of long underwear, rag-wool socks, the wind-proofness of the coveted boiled wool jacket I finally sprung for in a downtown shop, the absolute necessity of a scarf to cover my face when the wind chill dips too low for exposed skin to be safe.

As the deep cold wanes, my world is full of melting snow and the sometimes overwhelming smell of cow manure from the thawing fields around us. We're nearing the end of an academic semester. The desire to escape is strong. We all want a break from the cold, from dirty snowbanks, icy puddles, and the interminable reading and paper writing.

There are plenty of students whose families are sponsoring

them on trips to exotic warm locations but mine is not one of them. Same for many of my friends.

Sitting in a dorm room one night listening to Jimmy Buffett sing about boat drinks and cabin fever, and perhaps fueled by a few beers or a recent round at a downtown college hangout, someone says, "WE COULD! We could go!"

There's a pile of muddy snow boots outside the door, soggy coats hanging on hooks, skis piled behind the door of this cinder block room with the ubiquitous East Indian tapestries and rock star posters on the walls. The hallway carpet emits a faint smell of stale beer. The outdoor temps are still far from warm. Our student budgets for travel are zilch. Our situation definitely seems to put warmth in the realm of the impossible.

Dejected by how far out of reach our dreams of tropical islands are, someone shouts out a dejected, "What are you *talking* about? We can't go to the tropics."

"No, stupid! *Florida*. Not to The Keys, Buffett's hangout. That's way too far. But Daytona! Ft. Lauderdale! You can drive there from here in 24 hours if you share the driving and don't stop much. Ahhh! Can't you just feel it? Toes in the sand? Warm air? People, let's hear it for boat drinks!"

He does seem to have a point. And a car. In fact, three people in the room have cars. And desperation. With the clink of a few beer bottles, a plan is born.

Since I'm there at the planning and since one of the drivers is my boyfriend, I'm in. I have a ride to Florida for spring break.

But I have a different plan than the rest of them.

"Hello?" May answers the phone.

This is a delicious phone call to make. I haven't seen May and Billy since my high school graduation last spring, almost a year ago.

"Hey you sweet thing you," she says to me. "How are you doing?"

"Hi, May! I'm great. How are you? I'm wondering—will you and Billy be in Florida at the condo in April?"

"Well! We certainly will. Tell me you're going to come see me!"

I hear the hope and excitement in her voice.

"Yes, I am!"

"Oh, Shug!"

I know she's tap dancing on the kitchen carpet, right on that scorch mark where I accidentally dropped a hot iron years ago.

"You know you can come see me anytime!"

We start making plans to do the things we've always done together at the beach whether it's the two of us, the three of us, or a whole crowd of family —sit by the pool and take chairs down to the beach, dig our feet into the sand, watch waves roll in, watch the sandpipers tiptoe by and pelicans dive into the sea; take a trip to Marshall's or the mall to shop for clothes and shoes; ride down the beach at Daytona with Cokes; ride down A-1-A to see The Tahiti, the beachside hotel we used to stay in during my childhood. Wave to The Hawaiian Inn, my favorite spot for the hula show when I was younger.

Sometimes we drive over the high bridge up and over the Intracoastal Waterway, pointing out the view back towards the sea on one side and towards old downtown Daytona on the other where there are buildings and hotels in the Art Deco style. We like to go home on John Anderson Boulevard on the west side of the ICW where we drive slowly through the fancy neighborhoods, some houses gated with tall black wrought-iron across the driveway, lush gardens and live oak trees thick with sphagnum moss. Further north on John Anderson, some areas are still wild and swampy. We slow to watch heron wade through the still water.

This trip turns out to be no different than any other—I

come inside the cool condo late in the afternoon after a day at the beach. My skin is sticky with humidity, stiff with salt from the sea. My face is sun-touched. I've been outside all day in the water and the sand. Now it's time to wash it all away. May and I shower and primp. This is pretty simple for me since I'm mostly wash and wear. But I do put on a little mascara, some lipstick, some earrings. And I find a fun bright skirt to wear.

From May's bathroom, I smell minty Colgate toothpaste, hairspray. Her portable radio plays quietly and she hums along. She comes dancing out of her bedroom and into mine, showing off a new skirt, her hips swaying, her arms high like she's doing the hula.

"Don't you look adorable!" she tells me. I could be dressed in a rag and she'd say so.

"Don't YOU look adorable!" I say back.

Mostly dinner is out. Billy likes to announce he's cooking which means we're going out. He cooks every night at the beach.

We go to old favorites. A seafood restaurant we've gone to for years where I always get fried shrimp; another small place north of Daytona called Saltwater Cowboys that is in a low, weathered wooden building on the edge of a salt marsh. A small deck hangs out over the water outside where we sit and wait for our table while peepers sing their evening song under a pink and orange sunset. Here I mostly eat boiled shrimp and hushpuppies. The hushpuppies are the highlight of the meal here—perfectly seasoned and fried to a brown crisp on the outside while remaining tender on the inside. A hushpuppy is best described as a fried ball of savory cornbread batter. They are frequently served as a side dish to seafood in the South. The description doesn't do justice to their deliciousness.

Finally the hostess calls our name. Our table is ready!

"Walk this way," the hostess says.

Pretending to take her words as instruction, May does a tiny flouncy walk with one hand tucked up under her chin, a saucy turn to her cheek. We follow and all do a miniature imitation of her walk-this-way strut. Then we straighten up and behave, our hostess none the wiser.

When I first imagined telling my friends about my plans for the week in Florida I wasn't sure what sort of reaction to expect. Opting out of the party scene would not come as any surprise to them. They already knew it wasn't my thing and accepted that. But I was about to tell them that not only did I want to opt out of the party scene, I also wanted to opt out of the week entirely—to spend it with my grandmother and grandfather.

When I eventually told my friends, I didn't get any flak for it —but it wouldn't have mattered to me if I had. Spending time with May and Billy was way more important than the risk of embarrassment.

The week turns out to be just what I want and need—sleep, good food, sun and sand, and nurturing time among my family. I hope my friends are having fun, but I do not miss them or wonder if I'm missing out. I'm exactly where I want to be.

50

THE ONE ABOUT A BUDDING ROMANCE

When Ma Hawk took two-year-old Wea Wea to visit newly born Bud, Wea Wea announced she was going to marry him.

And she did.

51

SECRET WEAPON

I f Coca Cola is the sacred drink, lipstick is the magic
wand, the thing you put on to ward off trouble, to
summon courage, to literally and figuratively assist in
putting your best face forward. Even when—especially when—
you don't feel like it. Lipstick applied with intention is the secret
weapon, the battle flag flying.

A woman in my family can be down and out—in a hospital
bed, flat out with the flu, having relationship troubles or
grieving the death of a spouse. Life can suck, be full of lemons.
But the moment she says, "Bring me my lipstick," you better
watch out. It's game on. She's no longer going to take this lying
down. She may feel like crap, but she has tapped something
inside of herself. She's got intention now, whatever it may be.
The steel magnolia has been summoned. She's found her
ground, her center. She's got her story, and she's sticking to it.

When my mother says to me, "Time to put your lipstick on,"
I know I've just been instructed to find my big girl panties and
put them on. It's a subtle way of her telling me, "You've got
this," that it's time to get back on the horse. She's reminding me
of the strength that lives inside, telling me to reach down and

find that woman who doesn't take shit, who doesn't accept no for an answer, who is insightful and wise. Who *knows*. It's a reminder to find my voice again, to listen hard to what's rising up from inside, to trust myself and to remember the long line of women who came before me.

There's a meme with a photo of a young girl wearing a tiara. She has her eyes closed, head tilted up slightly, and she looks satisfied, peaceful. It says, "On the darkest days, when I feel inadequate, unloved and unworthy, I remember whose daughter I am, and straighten my crown." Or, in my case, I put on my lipstick.

52

VISITING GRANNY

After a series of debilitating strokes, Billy and May moved Billy's mother, Granny, to a nursing home outside Milledgeville. I was probably between eight and ten when she moved there. When I visited May and Billy, Billy would always say, "You should go visit Granny."

I *hated* going to visit her. First, she no longer had any idea who I was, and she wasn't much fun even when she had known me. She was notoriously grouchy and I never had much of a relationship with her.

But the real issue was that the nursing home terrified me. All these old people slumped in wheelchairs in the hallways or propped in beds staring vacantly out their doors. Or the ones who wanted to touch me when I walked by.

And the smell. Urine. Brokenness. Overcooked green beans and Brussels sprouts. Stale air and minds.

I told May how much I hated it. I wasn't able to come up with more words than that—just: "I hate it." It was fear—of death and languishing—and no way to cope with the sadness I saw there.

She pulled me in close for a hug. "Oh, Shug. I know. And I know what we'll do."

～

The next time Billy told us we should go, May said, "Yes we will. We'll go to Chaplinwood."

And we did. Go to Chaplinwood. But when we got there, May got out of the car and said to me, "Shug, you stay right here. I'll be back in a jiffy."

Ten minutes later she was back and gave me the report. Granny had had her hair styled, had a new house dress, and was doing fine.

When Billy asked later that evening if we had gone, May didn't miss a beat.

"Yes, we went to Chaplinwood." Technically true.

"Didn't we?"

Yes, I nodded.

"And Granny had a haircut and a new dress and she looked great."

Case closed.

I never actually saw Granny again. But I sure went to Chaplinwood a lot over the years.

53

PERFECT

People have asked me if May was really that perfect.

Yes.

No.

Did she drive people crazy at times?

Yes. Don't we all?

I could see, as I got older, the things she did that weren't in her best interest. Perhaps she overused the it's-easier-to-get-forgiveness-than-permission approach. She did not ever love those brought into the family (think husbands and wives) quite as much as those of us born in. She could be judgmental—like all of us. She could never find her car keys. She was not a great cook, despite her interest in food and her large collection of recipes.

But none of us are perfect. Who knows what I did as a child —or an adult, for that matter—that annoyed her. Whatever it was, she did not point it out. Neither of us were perfect. *But we were perfect for one another.* Our relationship was perfect *for us.*

The world would be an infinitely better place if everyone had someone like May. Someone who loves you more than life itself.

54

FIRE ALARM

Transcribed from a letter to me from May, undated

"This is something worth writing you
about -
You know I told you I had planned
on cooking the sausage for my dinner
to nite - well- - - I had already
let some cube steak thaw (out) - so
I said OK it's cube steak - as I was
making some dark gravy to go over
my grits - the smoke alarm sounded
off - & my answering machine was shouting - (You)
(Idiot) - Fire, Fire, Fire - (which)
(I know) - I was the only one cooking -
so about that time the phone rang and
the Fire dept said they had a truck
on the way - I said "No!" - keep
him With You - she said look out of
your door & you'll see them - then a
police car drove up - well all I

said - I don't cook very much - & this
proves I shouldn't - - - - - but wouldn't
you like to have some Steak! - They
refused and ran up the drive as fast as
they could - (to get away from me the
maniac Idiot - The steak was delicious
exciting too!) I yelled to them "be careful
you might hurt yourself - Last thing I saw
they were throwing there (sic) arms in the air"

55

I KNOW WHERE I WAS STANDING

I'm not sure if May started to change or if I was just older and started to be able to recognize it, but she could get crabby, annoyed, and she'd strike out at others. Usually I was immune—but not always. Often she wouldn't let Billy talk or finish his story. She'd be impatient with his telling or perhaps somehow embarrassed or put off by it and she'd take over or say, with a sigh, *"Oh, Billy!"*

For as long as I can remember, she couldn't keep track of her car keys, something that mystified me. Even as a child, my mind worked in a way that made the solution obvious. All you had to do was make a decision, decide where your keys "lived," and always put them there. I tried to kindly school her in this approach, with no apparent success.

Often we'd come home from errands or shopping, hauling armfuls of bags into the house. Later, unable to find something —a book, a new pair of pants or her keys—she'd look at one of us and ask if we knew where they were.

"No—sorry, haven't seen them."

Frustrated, she'd put her hands on her hips, cock her head,

purse her lipsticked lips and claim, "I know where I was standing when I saw you with them!"

The misplacement of things was usually someone else's fault, and she did not apologize when it became clear none of us had absconded with her item. But we didn't argue or get mad about it. We just shrugged and chalked it up to May being May.

I will also say I understand this better now. I sheepishly admit to wanting to blame others for missing items before turning the spotlight on myself. Now that the kids have flown the coop, Adam and I joke about no longer being able to blame them when we can't find our stuff.

Recently, I was talking to Mom on the phone, telling her I couldn't find a cookbook she had given me a few years ago.

"I know it's in this house because I saw it recently. But now I can't find it . . . but I know where you were standing, holding it in your hand the last time I saw it," I said to her.

She just laughed.

This frequently happens when one of us can't find something. With a smile, we turn to the other: "I know where you were standing... ." It's a little remembrance, a way May stays with us. It is our own form of ancestor worship, to call up the stories, the peculiarities, the sometimes annoying but also endearing quirks. It is the way we keep each other close, no matter the distance between us.

56

THE ONE ABOUT THE VEIL

Wea Wea was well into her later years, with adult children, when this gem occurred. She attended the Methodist Church, her family church. But one Sunday she went to a friend's church with her to meet the new minister there. Milledgeville was a small town and newcomers were interesting.

She dressed in her Sunday best, including a hat with a net veil that hung down over the face just below the nose, the fashion at the time.

Wea Wea and her friend sat through the service and then stood in the winding line up the aisle out of the church to where the minister was greeting parishioners on the front steps. She was chewing gum. Just as she and her friend reached the minister and began to speak with him, Wea Wea got her veil caught in her mouth and stuck to her gum. She reasoned she couldn't spit it out because she'd be left standing there with a wad of chewing gum hanging from the bottom of her veil. So she just kept chewing.

"I just near 'bout had to eat that whole veil," she told me.

57

MISS ME

May died on the twenty-eighth of May 2012 after a number of years of increasing confusion and dementia. I was fifty years old. Mostly she still seemed to know who I was but as time passed and we talked on the phone, she would frequently confuse me with my cousin, her other grand-daughter, calling me Bridget. It was okay. And not that far off from most of her life when, as many mothers and grandmothers, she would often run through the list of family names trying to land on the right one. I was always happy to answer to whatever she called me. I knew she was addressing me. She could call me Bridget, Suzanne, Betty, Margie, Ricky, Billy, Kathy. I'd answer.

Even in those years when she wasn't so clear in her thinking, I still loved picking up the phone just to hear her voice. I could see her in my mind, doing that little thing she'd do when she was excited about something. I could imagine her doing a little mini step-step with her feet, a happy dance as she answered the phone, saying to me, "Oh, Shug! It's so *good* to hear you!"

I'd tell her about what I'd been doing, about work, the dogs, our adventures, travel and, once they came along, lots of stories about the kids. She'd tell me about her latest decorating plans, what she'd been eating, about her new favorite songs, who she'd been to lunch with, whether she'd been getting her exercise by walking.

After her funeral, Uncle Ricky was walking out of the church with three year-old Will, his grandchild and one of May's great-grandchildren. As Will held Ricky's hand and walked down the front steps, Will looked up.

"Where's May?" he asked.

"She's not here anymore, Will. She's gone to heaven."

There was a long silence as Will took this in. Finally he looked up at Ricky.

"Well, she sure is going to miss me," he said seriously.

"She sure is," Ricky told him.

58

RED BUTTE CEMETERY

My mom called recently to tell me she'd decided to buy a cemetery plot at Red Butte Cemetery in Aspen, CO where she's lived for the past 40 years, where I spent my last few teenage years, and one of the places I call home. Then she asked me if I'd like to buy one too. I'd never thought about buying a cemetery plot. I mean *ever*. It seemed like a weird thing to do. Like something *other* people did. People in novels. Or old people. Or people I don't know. People over there. But not something I'd do.

Plus, I always figured I'd be cremated. But even before her phone call, I'd been rethinking this a bit. Not the cremation part. That part is clear to me. The thought of being placed in a coffin and buried in a hole is claustrophobic to me in a way that being burned to ashes and cinder is not. I know this is wholly irrational in both cases, seeing as I'd already be dead, but there it is.

But as you now know, I love the history and stories cemeteries hold.

And then there was a recent drive Adam and I took through

the Red Butte Cemetery. True friends were there—a few people I had gone to high school with (*He died?*) and many other members of the community I had known over the years (*Oh, I remember her!*). To drive through the cemetery was to reconnect with people, to remember them, to have them brought to mind.

I liked that. I liked "seeing" these people I knew. I liked knowing where they were. I liked the trip down memory lane I got just by driving through and seeing their names, plus the other people I've gotten to know and get to know better each time I walk through there with Mom.

All those experiences, plus recently seeing photos of a gravestone of a great-great-grand-someone of mine in a cemetery in New Hampshire made me think I didn't want to scatter myself to the wind. Cremated, yes. But put to rest somewhere specific. Someplace I can point to from my very alive life now, someplace I know I'll be. And I like knowing where my mom will be. Just like I thought the buying of burial plots was a little weird, I also never imagined myself being drawn to visit a loved one in a cemetery. Which now that I say it seems odd since I like visiting all those other people I didn't even know in life.

It's the sense of continuity or something like that. A touchstone for a life that was. A record. I wonder about the lack of records we'll leave behind in the digital age: no letters, maybe even fewer photos since so much is kept now in the digital space.

I said yes to my mom. A plot right next to hers, where Adam and I can be buried side-by-side. In Aspen, Colorado, the place where I declared at age seventeen I was sure my soul had been born.

At the risk of continuing to reveal this cemetery weirdness, now when I go to see Mom in Aspen, one of the must-do's is to go to the cemetery, visit our plots, look out over the valley, hear the creek rushing below, visit graves that are now becoming favorites. It makes me oddly content to know that this place, my soul place, and right next to my mama and Adam, is where I will spend eternity.

59

HANDS

One of the times I miss May the most is when I'm cooking dinner and sipping wine. I often used to call her then for a short visit, just to be held by her voice, to hear her endearments, to hear her say "stay sweet" when we said goodbye. I'd stand at my kitchen counter, chopping vegetables, stirring a pot, gazing out the window waiting for water to boil. Wherever she was in her house, I could imagine her, see all the details, this house I'd known my entire life. Most often she was in her bedroom, her little TV or radio playing quietly in the background while she talked to me.

I was at the Great Sand Dunes National Monument in southern Colorado, camping with the kids in May 2009 when May broke her hip and had a small stroke 2000 miles away in Georgia.

Now, she and the Sand Dunes are always connected for me. They give me a lump in my throat. The beauty and miraculousness of that place and their bigness paired with the bigness of beginning to lose her and the miracle of her unconditional love.

I stood there looking out at the impossible landscape, 30

square miles of sand dunes, some of them 750 feet tall, flanked by the snow covered peaks of the Sangre de Christo mountain range. Surrounded by dramatic, improbable beauty, my kids delirious with the freedom of camping life— no demands to brush their teeth, allowed to wipe their hands on their pants with abandon, and free to get as dirty as possible—I felt shaky inside, wobbly, knowing a solid part of my world was coming unmoored.

We hiked to a waterfall, the trail rocky, dusty and dry. As I put one foot in front of the other and listened to the clink of stones under my feet, tears rolled down my cheeks. It felt good to walk, to move, because there was nothing else I could do. I was far away and it was all out of my hands.

Adam was riding his motorcycle down to the Dunes to meet us the day I learned May wasn't doing well. He was supposed to text when he left Boulder, and again when he got to Buena Vista, CO, halfway there.

I didn't hear from him, and my mind started doing that thing I try not to let it do—run down the road of doom, of him somewhere by the side of the road on a mangled motorcycle. When I finally heard from him, all was fine and he had just forgotten. But all wasn't fine inside of me.

My heart was breaking as my grandmother, my greatest love and constant cheerleader, was breaking down.

Years after May is gone, I look at my own hands and see the same crepey skin I used to love on the backs of her hands, and her mother's hands, and my own mom's. I remember rubbing my fingers lightly over it, gently pushing on the blue veins that stood out.

When I first notice my own wrinkly blue-veined skin, I recoil and think it looks like old-people skin. But then I remember hands looking just like this, hands I love more than anything on earth. I vow to love and honor my own aging hands for the people who will love them the same way.

Hands that connect me to my Mom, to May, to Betty and Wea Wea, to all the hands that have held me, patted me on the back, feathered bangs over my forehead. All the hands that have taken me in for hugs, removed tangles from my hair, righted a twisted sock on my small foot. Hands laid gently on my brow checking for fever, hands held while crossing the street, hands that caught me as I entered this world and all the hands that held me afterwards. Hands that tickled and scratched my back, hands that painted Christmas ornaments with me, hands that spooned food into my mouth, hands that prepared that food. Hands, one on each cheek, as a kiss is delivered.

Hands. All the hands that have held me. Especially her hands.

60

FROG

Once with Mom and May, visiting a cousin in Virginia, I caught a frog. I must have been about five years old. I loved this frog and wanted to take it back to May's house in Georgia. May didn't bat an eyeball.

She found a shoebox. We picked grass and put it in the bottom. We had water for the frog. I'm not sure how we fed it. We drove back to Milledgeville with it. Periodically, I'd tell May it needed some air and she'd roll down the window and hold him up so he could enjoy the breeze.

Miraculously, the frog survived the trip and days of handling by small hands. One day I took him out onto the terrace to show him the lake behind May and Billy's house. It must have looked inviting because the frog tried to jump. I didn't want to lose him. Plus, it was a long way down into the shrubs from the terrace. I didn't want him to get hurt in the fall.

So I squeezed. Too hard. It wasn't a good end for my beloved but nameless frog.

I haven't picked up a frog since.

61

HOG MONUMENT

One night about six years ago, I opened an email from my mom, one she had forwarded to me from a childhood friend of hers from Milledgeville.

The subject line was "Hog Monument." Well, *that* caught my attention. It's not often I get emails about monuments or hogs.

The body of the email went something like this: The writer said he and his wife had recently visited a place called The Pig Monument just outside a tiny town called Oconee, about 25 miles from Milledgeville, after seeing an article about it in Milledgeville's local paper. Oconee is near a town called Tennille, which is a family name, the last name of Wea Wea and Bud.

The email went on to say my mom's name—Suzanne Caskey—and her mom's name—May Donnelly—were both engraved on the stone among the list of donors. "Scroll down," the writer suggested, "to the photo I've attached and see if you can read the names."

∼

The stone, six feet tall and about four feet wide reads: "On this spot in 1933 during the Great Depression neighbors of a farmer named Bartow Barron joined together to rescue his pig from a dry well. This monument is erected to the spirit of friendship and community so characteristic of those times."

Here's the story as recounted by Wesley Pittman, when he was interviewed at age ninety-four by Milledgeville's Union Recorder newspaper: When he was eight years old in 1933, he lived on a farm next to Mr. Barron, when Barron's prize and only pig went missing. It being the Depression, and Barron being a small farmer, the loss of his one and only pig, the one he was depending on to provide his winter's worth of meat, was a serious loss. Barron searched and searched for his pig with no luck.

Finally Barron returned to the site of a 40-foot deep dry well on his property—and now the site of the memorial—and there, gazing at him from the depths—was his skinny, hungry, decidedly stranded pig.

The story goes that Bartow started throwing scraps down to the pig and lowered water to the animal in a bucket to keep the pig alive while he figured out how to extract it.

Reportedly, a well cleaner in North Carolina had the equipment required to reach that far down to reach the stuck animal, but he wouldn't be available for months. Neither Barron or the pig had that long to wait.

Barron scratched his head. Now what?

In what I regard as a stroke of genius, he decided to start slowly filling the well with dirt until the level was high enough the pig could be reached. But you can imagine how many shovelfuls of dirt it would take to fill a 40-foot deep well. He wasn't going to be able to do it alone.

The tale of Barron and his well-bound pig spread. People came from near and far to help shovel dirt down into the well.

This included the then eight year-old Wesley Pittman, Wesley's father, friends, acquaintances, and total strangers.

Barron kept feeding and watering his pig while shovelfuls of dirt were tossed into the well, slowly by slowly raising the level of the well and thereby the pig. A very slow dirt elevator.

It took twelve days. But finally the pig stepped out of the well, back above ground. It had been a true community effort. People reportedly came from all around, on foot, by horse, by mule-pulled wagon and by Model T, to talk, to watch, to help and to take in the spectacle of a pig rescue.

It seems like it ended well for the pig but, alas, some reports have it that the pig survived his adventure only to be put to his intended purpose. If the story is to be trusted, the pig was slaughtered, roasted, helpers were fed and feted, and Bartow Barron still had food for the winter.

At the very bottom of the marker, in italic script, there's a footnote: "See H. Lawrence *Southland and Other Poems of the South* 1992 pp. 11-12."

H. Lawrence is Reverend Harold Lawrence, retired Methodist minister whose next to last assignment from 1990-2004 was at Milledgeville's First Methodist Church. Besides being a minister, he is the author of narrative poetry and stories about the South. While writing his book *Southland and Other Stories of the South*, Lawrence heard the story of Barron and his pig, inspiring the poem "The Depression Pig," referenced on the footnote of the memorial.

Pittman, a parishioner at First Methodist, was able to fill Lawrence in on the details.

At some point, something inspired Lawrence to build a monument to the pig and the community of people who pitched in to save it. People from Lawrence's congregation supported the effort and the pig memorial was born.

~

I scroll down to the photo of the monument attached to the email, interested in seeing my mom's and grandmother's names carved into an unlikely memorial for a Depression-era pig. I scan the inscription. Then my eyes move down the face of the stone to where the word "Donors" is centered above three columns of names. I start scanning down the first column.

The first column: Beegee Baugh. Ah, yes. Wife of Dr. Baugh, the pediatrician credited with saving my young life when I was oh so sick. May Donnelly, my maternal grandmother. Charles Ennis. Familiar name. Noel Fowler. Possibly related to me as there are Fowlers in my family. Then, wait! What!? Chris Chandler. That's MY name! My name is on the memorial as a donor. I burst out laughing.

"What?" my husband asks.

"My name! It's on a PIG memorial!"

He gives me a blank stare. I hand him my phone with the photo enlarged, my name, second to last in the first column of donors.

How my name ended up there I'm not quite sure. But I can come up with a very good guess. Harold lived next door to May. I imagine May heard about the effort from Harold himself, possibly over a martini, which I've heard from a reliable source, they sometimes shared, Harold arriving with all the ingredients and a precise recipe.

It probably went like this: May found out from Harold, or neighbors, or the local paper, or likely all of the above. A woman with a sense of humor and fun and great regard for The Preacher Next Door, as she often referred to Harold, it's no surprise she embraced the idea of donating.

I would have been thirty years old when the monument was erected. Its dedication was in October 1992.

I imagine myself sitting in my living room in Southwest Washington State, a wood fire blazing against the damp cool, two dogs at my feet. Or cooking dinner with a small glass of white wine at hand, talking to her on the phone as I often did when I prepared dinner.

She would have still been living in her home next to Harold, the blue jays squawking overhead in the pines, fighting over the stale bread she often threw off the back stoop for them. She was probably back in her bedroom, TV on quietly, or the radio playing.

I can hear her laughing, feel myself laughing on the other end, at the craziness of it, the weirdness, which made it that much more appealing. And deciding to support the cause of memorializing a pig. Or maybe she offered to donate for me, something she would do. Just because.

That, I suppose, is how my name, along with my mom's and May's, ended up on a monument to a pig twenty or so feet off of State Route 272, pretty much in the middle of nowhere in Washington County, Georgia.

I couldn't be more proud.

62

HOME PLACE

Home. Place. What it means to belong. The home place. That's how my dad refers to the farm outside Milledgeville, GA where his mother grew up, a place he continued to visit as a child. A place my great aunt continued to live and that I also have vague memories of. A white farmhouse, pecan trees, rough fields.

In the past few years as I write these stories, I've been asking my family to fill in the holes, fill in the gaps in the stories I've heard about both sides of my southern family for my entire life. Stories I ask for again and again, ones that make up the scrap quilt of understanding who I am, where I came from.

I left the home place long ago and found a new home, a place my soul also recognized as mine. And yet, I haven't forgotten the home place and the people that populate it. It tugs on my mind, asks me to feel the texture of the quilted squares of memory, to follow the threads, to feel the hands of those who stitched them. Some essence inside me, photographic negatives burned into my body. The past, the one I experienced physically and through stories, the one I saw in pictures. It still lives today. It tells me who I am, where I came from, where I belong. The home place.

My physical return to the home place is infrequent. But my heart returns there often—my morning grits with lots of butter put me back at my spot at Grandmother and Granddaddy Chandler's big dining room table; the roasted Georgia pecans my dad cooks and sends on Christmas and my birthday remind me of driving by acres of pecan groves; of the pecan trees that dropped nuts in our side yard in Texas and how we'd stomp on them on the sidewalk and pick the meat out; talking to my family on the phone and asking to be told a familiar story carries me back to every tale told when my family gathers together; lingering to listen to a stranger's southern accent wraps me in arms of love; the longing to reach for the phone while cooking dinner to talk to May like I did when she was alive keeps her here with me as I chop vegetables and hear her voice in my head, saying, "Oh, Shug!"; drinking a Coca-Cola while driving down the road with the windows open and the radio playing fills my car with the spirit of my mom, May, Betty, Kathy, Margie, Wea Wea, all of my ancestors, known and unknown.

These are the things that tether me to the connection and memories. My touchstones of home.

THANK YOU

Thank you for taking the time to read my stories. I hope your time in these pages has brought you comfort, joy, laughter, and a sense of being held in love. I also hope these stories have given you an appreciation for your own stories. Storytelling leads us to connection with one another, so I hope you'll be encouraged to share yours, too.

For information on my writing circles, to read my blog, and to stay connected, please visit my website at www.WritingUnleashed.net.

Love, love,
Chris

Please review my book on **Amazon** amzn.to/3GZSnFk and Goodreads.com. Your reviews help other readers find my book and your feedback means the world to me.

ACKNOWLEDGMENTS

They say it takes a village to raise a child. The same is true for birthing and raising a book. I have been supported by *so* many people.

None of this, of course, would have been possible without its inspiration and my greatest cheerleader, my grandmother, May Tennille Donnelly. And the rest of my lovely and, yes, quirky family who carry the tradition and the stories; the people who raised a storyteller, who NEVER say no when I ask for a family story, and who always knew I could do it, whatever "it" was. My love affair with words began at the knees of these people. Thanks to Margie and Ricky Donnelly, aunt and uncle extraordinaire, keepers of the stories, and for their willingness to dig through boxes of photos when I call to ask for a decades old picture.

My mom, Suzanne Donnelly Caskey, furthered the love of words by putting books into my hands and helped me become a reader. My life would be vastly dimmer without stories and words. And without her.

Thanks to my dad, Jimmy Chandler, who has been steadfast in his encouragement and curiosity about my writing. And to my stepmom, Hardy Chandler, or as I prefer, "other Mom," who has been equally enthusiastic.

Without realizing it, I started writing this book many years ago in my first writing group with a small circle of friends in my then-home of Ridgefield, Washington—Karen Beall, Ailsa Crawford, Jan Healy, Marie Camille Lentsch. It was at kitchen tables with these women that the stories first started tumbling out onto the page.

Certainly this book would not exist without my current Boulder writing group. I would be nowhere without their cheers, laughter, tears, hand holding, hugs, and wise and kind feedback. Jennifer Rhode, Cait McQuade, Christine Tracy, there are not enough words to thank you for your generous and encouraging spirits.

When I got serious about turning my random stories into a cohesive narrative, Boulder's Tanja Pajevic and her Memoir Mastermind class provided a container that kept me writing, crafting and shaping, and supported my evolving vision of this book. An offshoot of the Mastermind group morphed into the Daredevil Writers and reinforced the value of setting tiny weekly goals I couldn't possibly fail to meet. Thanks, Nicole Harkin, for being the inspiration for the Daredevils, and for being our fearless leader and Queen of Writing Resources— even if you are sometimes in the bathtub when it's time to write (well, okay, only once!). Sandi Phinney, Cindy Powell, Jessica Stokes, Jennifer Gore, and Christy Nedrow. And again, Christine Tracy, for being the uber-handholder and encourager.

To Suzette Mullen, amazing book coach of Your Story Finder, who kept saying, "More May!"

To Laurie Wagner, my Wild Writing mentor. And to my Wild Writing sisters especially Joyce Belcher, Tanya Shaffer, Tanya Pearlman, Sheila Bannon and, again, my mom.

Thanks to my beta readers, Sheridan Wolfe (also for her crafting and walking enthusiasm), Nicole Harkin, Cait McQuade, and Ruth Blaw. Also Ruth because she's been there since the early days and she "gets" it all.

There are people who I want to thank simply because they are the ones who help me get through the day—Lisa Stevens, to whom I send text rants, photos of bad fashion, and random thoughts about my day. I can (and do) show my worst self to her and she doesn't judge. Kim Decker, who has supported me through, not only a black belt in To Shin Do, but in parenting teenagers, which earns us a black belt in and of itself.

To Buddy, Sugarplum and Queso, our dogs who kept me company during these writing years. They slept under my desk, kept my feet warm, and provided moral support in a way only dogs can (the barking was *not* helpful—but no one is perfect). Since I do my best thinking, gain the most clarity, and come up with the best ideas while moving, they get a whole lot of credit because they keep me walking and moving EVERY day. When I'm stuck, the best thing to do is go for a walk. They are always willing companions.

To my son, Levi, who placed dibs on the first signed copy. To my son, Oliver, who has been equally supportive and whose wordplay and puns make me laugh. My life would not be the same without boy humor, which I've come to love and enjoy more than I would have imagined. To Miyu, my bonus daughter, who rubs my shoulders as I sit at my desk and asks, "Mom, how is your book going?"

Last and absolutely not least, my husband, Adam Baker, who has faith in my writing even when I do not. He always reminded me I could do this. Thanks for being my partner on this wild and lovely ride.

ABOUT THE AUTHOR

Chris Chandler is a storyteller, author, and book lover. She is a two-time cast member of Boulder's Listen To Your Mother show and has been published on ScaryMommy.com and in The Boulder Magazine. She lives in Boulder, CO with her husband, is the mother of two sons and one bonus daughter. She helps others find and tell their stories by facilitating writing circles for women.

Her website is www.WritingUnleashed.net.
linktr.ee/chrischandler

RED THREAD BOOKS

Red Thread Publishing is an all-female publishing company on a mission to support 10,000 women to become successful published authorpreneurs & thought leaders.

To work with us or connect regarding any of our growing library of books email us at **info@redthreadbooks.com**.
To learn more bout us visit our website
www.redthreadbooks.com.

Follow us & join the community.

www.ingramcontent.com/pod-product-compliance
Lightning Source LLC
Chambersburg PA
CBHW031044160726
47991CB00005B/2019